AF327906

Essentials
of
Underwater
Photography

By
Robert M. Jackson

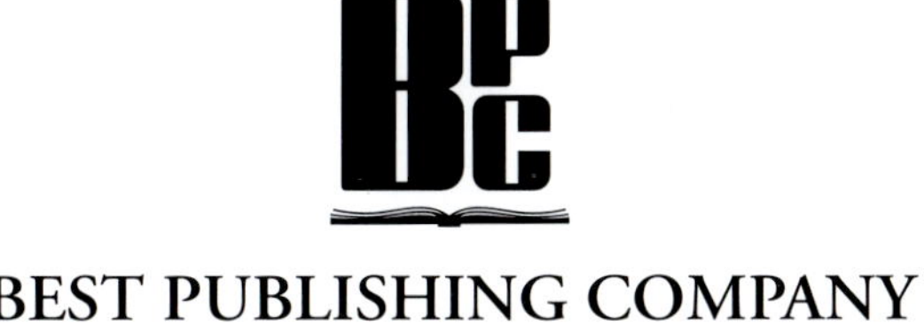

BEST PUBLISHING COMPANY

Photography by Robert M. Jackson
Photo of Author by Joel Silverstein

Edited by Andy Nordhoff
Layout by Dawña Argenbright

ISBN 0-941332-77-2
Library of Congress Catalog Number 99-61589

Printed in Hong Kong

Best Publishing Company
2355 North Steves Boulevard
P.O. Box 30100
Flagstaff, AZ 86003-0100 USA

For Nat and Emily...

TABLE OF CONTENTS

"Look. A man walks toward the sea. He bends over it, hands cupped. He stands erect and the water escapes through his tightly pressed fingers. He watches it flowing in the light."

Phillippe Tailliez, 1954, <u>To Hidden Depths</u>

Underwater photographers have produced many texts since the marine biologist Louis Boutan first made an underwater photograph in 1893. Each has filled a niche that I believe is important and interesting. Many of these books stimulated my early interest in underwater photography. They remain on my shelf and I refer to them with interest to this day.

Often I found the information in these books fascinating, but ultimately frustrating, because of the omission of critical details. Other times I found the presentation of straightforward and practical information obscured by generalizations or irrelevant (frequently wrong) theoretical explanations. My goal was to write a clear and simple photographers' manual based on my own experience. I have presented protocols that can be adapted to many different situations, whatever the equipment available.

As I have learned about underwater photography, I have tried to be open to new knowledge and apply that to my work. A Zen-like ability to achieve this receptive state is a rare gift that has not come to me often. The information I will convey has been obtained more often through mistakes and experience.

Some divers and photographers who preceded me have guided those experiences. I recognize especially Bob Mercer, who taught me to dive at the YMCA at age 15, and Kenneth R.H. Read, D.Sc. at Boston University, for opening a window to see beyond medical school. Many others have led me through a graduate school in the ocean.

For practical reasons and because of limits to my knowledge, the text is devoted almost exclusively to 35mm equipment. The emphasis is on housed 35mm cameras, especially Nikons, for which there exists a wide range of commercially available housings. Nikonos cameras have always defined underwater photography and eventually evolved into automated, submersible SLRs.

In essence, no camera does more than focus and control the light falling on a piece of film. To have artistic control, a photographer must only learn to use these two camera functions to express a personal vision of how light travels, reflects, and diffuses through water.

R. Jackson
2000

HISTORY

"The view of reality as an exotic prize to be tracked down and captured by the diligent hunter-with-a-camera has informed photography from the beginning, and marks the confluence of the Surrealist counter-culture and middle-class adventurism. Photography has always been fascinated by social heights and lower depths."

Susan Sontag, 1973, <u>On Photography</u>

The Beginnings of Underwater Photography

Underwater photography began in the late 19th century. Most authors attribute the birth of underwater photography to a Frenchman, Louis Boutan, but few have had access to his book, <u>La Photographie Sous-Marine</u>. Published in 1900, the marine zoologist's book described his wet plate camera and its heavy waterproof housing. His light source was an alcohol lamp in an oxygen-filled glass tube. Boutan blew explosive magnesium dust on the flame to create artificial light in order to make the exposure.

The camera used by Louis Boutan, a marine biologist, to produce some of the first underwater photographs. It was immobile because of the long exposures required by the slow emulsions used.

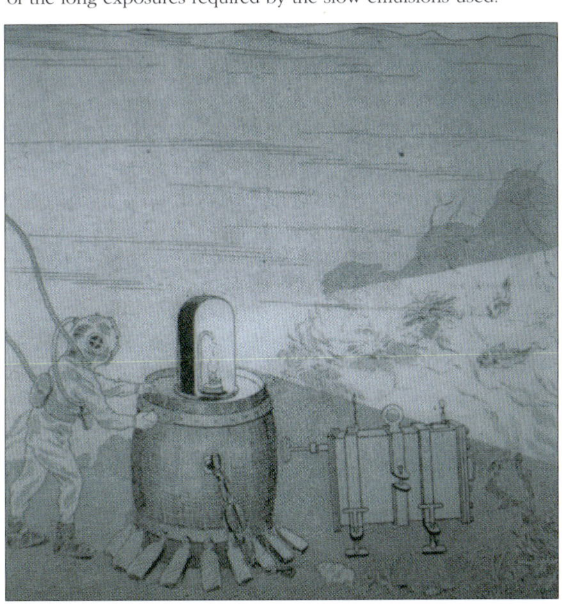

1

Only about thirty years later, *National Geographic* magazine published the first underwater color photographs, which were called Autochromes. Martin and Longley described their surface and underwater equipment and showed their results in a classic article that reproduced color photographs taken under water near Fort Jefferson in the Florida Keys.

Entering the Modern Era

As with most other aspects of underwater exploration, Jacques-Yves Cousteau popularized underwater photography after he and Emile Gagnan invented the demand regulator, the "Aqualung," in 1942. In the Silent World he described his attempts at making underwater 35mm movies during World War II in occupied France. The young diver obtained 35mm Leica film and spliced it into long pieces to produce moving pictures several minutes in length.

The Evolution of Modern Equipment

Underwater photography usually requires artificial light because absorption of light by water attenuates both color and contrast. Flash bulbs served this purpose, but like other archaic technologies, eventually succumbed to impracticality. The availability of underwater strobes stimulated U/W photography and made it an accessible art. Harold Edgerton, an electrical engineer and MIT faculty member, initially developed the strobe as a mechanism to produce very brief flashes of light. This, of course, is useful if you want to study rapidly moving objects like parts of machines. Dimitri Rebikoff refined these electronic flash units further. Miniaturization of the strobe and development of small, powerful batteries allowed its use underwater. The mass production of the strobe made the modern era of U/W photography possible. Edgerton described its development and use in a 1955 *National Geographic* article.

Luis Marden, a *National Geographic* photographer, presented important ideas regarding U/W photography in several articles published throughout the 1950s. He worked in the mercifully warm Indian Ocean making Kodachrome and Ektachrome images with medium format cameras and flashbulbs. The images are bold and colorful, even by today's very high standards. Marden is credited with defining many ideas prevalent in underwater photography today.

Equipment evolved at an increasingly rapid pace from the 1950s to today. Eventually, medium format cameras including the twin lens reflex

Rolleiflex SL found their way into precisely machined metal housings. Hans Hass, one of the fathers of modern diving, developed it in association with the German company Franke and Heidecke. The medium format, twin-lens reflex camera had inherent parallax problems, but the large viewfinder allowed fairly accurate focusing in low light. No O-rings were used in the original housing type. Flat gaskets, instead of O-rings, sealed the housing and control shafts.

The Cousteau team developed the Calypso camera, a proto-Nikonos that incorporated most of the features of its present day descendant. A Belgian engineer designed the small 35mm adjustable camera to be the underwater equivalent of a "miniature camera" like tourists carry. These evolved rapidly from the "Spiro Etanche" in 1960 to the "Calypso Phot/Nikonos" in 1963. Most recently, the Nikonos series has included the present Nikonos V (1989) and the autofocus, SLR Nikonos RS (1992).

Despite the success of the Nikonos cameras, more significant technical advances have come as housings for 35mm Nikon SLR cameras. Giddings-Felgen "Niko-Mar"

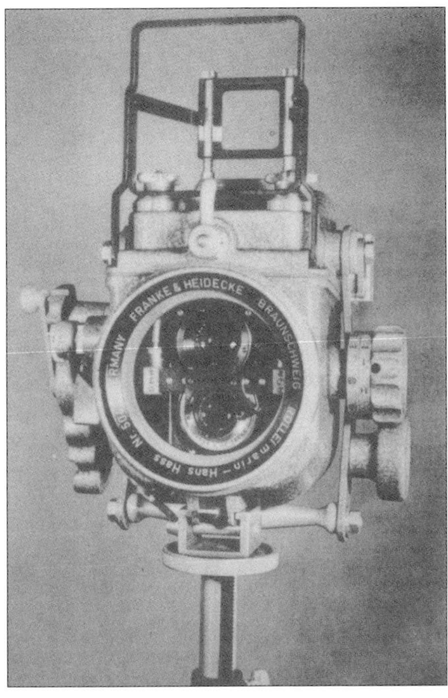

The Rolleimarin camera housing developed by Hans Hass. It housed the Rollei twin lens reflex camera, which provided a large viewfinder. Although limited in availability of lenses, it became standard for many years and was used extensively by Marden, Faulkner, and others.

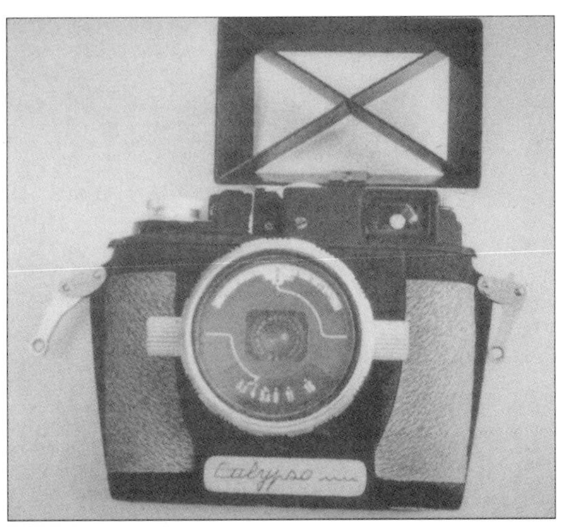

The Calypso camera popularized by Cousteau during the 1950s. It was the first waterproof miniature (35mm) camera marketed. The robust design remained essentially unchanged until the Nikonos IV camera with internal electronics was introduced.

was one of the earliest metal, dome port housings that allowed use of the Nikon F with its indispensable "Action Finder." This prototype of future housings permitted the photographer to use the wide range of Nikon lenses designed for above-water use. The Niko-Mar enabled the photographer to observe the full viewfinder image in a large rectified prism. The combination of these two features was so important, they have been incorporated into essentially all subsequent professional housings.

The next advance in housing design was the result of a collaboration between Bates Littlehales, a *National Geographic* photographer, and Gomer McNeil, an optical engineer. They designed a metal housing for the Nikon F, which was subsequently built and marketed by Mitchell Photogrammetry as the "Ocean Eye." This housing placed the lens in the optical center of a large hemispherical plexiglass port that eliminated the enlarging effect of water. So, a housed 28mm lens under water behaved like a 28mm lens in air. Fisheye lenses and split image, over-under shots

This fisheye photograph of my diving buddy was made years ago using "primitive" equipment. Despite that, the shot worked and still tells a story. **(Nikonos; Agfachrome 64; Nikonos flash with 25B blue bulb; Green Things accessory fisheye lens on Nikonos 35mm lens; 1/30 second at ƒ5.6)**

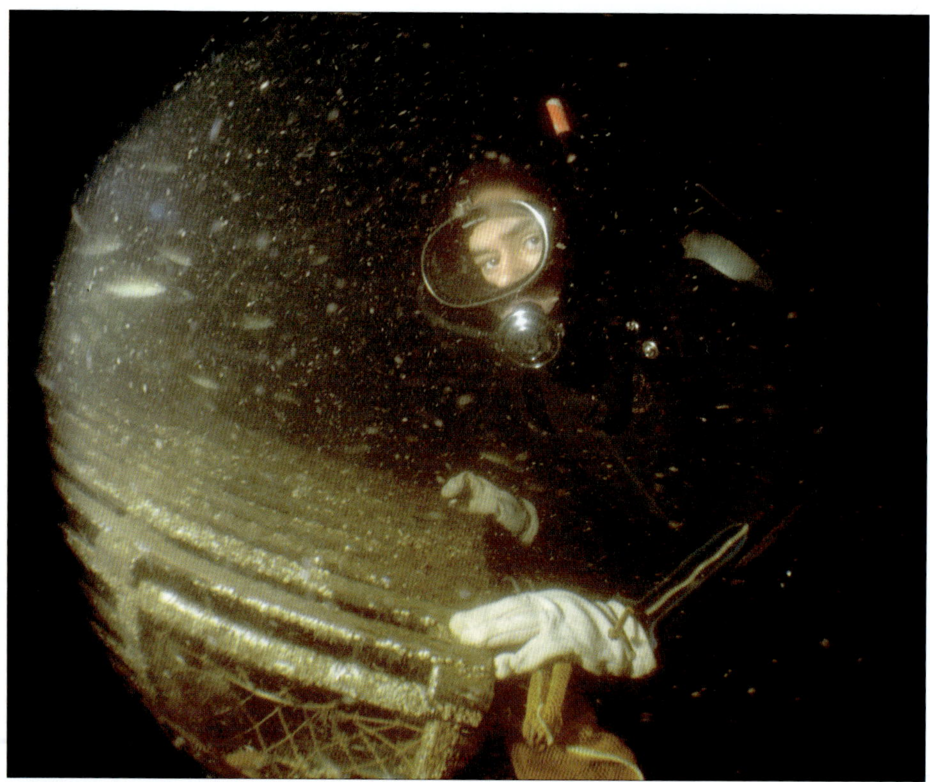

Essentials of Underwater Photography

suddenly became possible. Bob Hollis' company, Oceanic, also marketed a housing for the Nikon F series that incorporated some of these features. Some of these "Hydro 35" housings are still in use today. Rebuilt models are still marketed by Camera Tech in San Francisco, California.

More recently, Aqua-Vision Systems produced a line of metal housings for both Nikon and Canon cameras. Beginning with a model for the Nikon F3, the company has manufactured finely machined aluminum housings for the F4, 8008s, N90s, F5, and Canon F1.

Throughout this period, Ikelite produced a frequently modified Lucite housing that has been adapted to fit many cameras ranging from the Nikon F to the N90s. Light weight and relatively low cost characterize these classic Ikelite housings.

Several companies in Europe and Japan have recently recognized the small but dedicated market for high quality 35mm SLR housings. Subal, Hugyfot, Nexus, and several others now market F4, F5, or N90s housings for the advanced amateur or professional market. The underwater market remains small enough that the manufacturers compete based on quality rather than price.

The OceanEye 100 dome port housing marketed by Mitchell Photogrammetry, Inc. in the 1970s. The design was by Gomer McNeil and Bates Littlehales. It housed the Nikon F and all available Nikon lenses. The large dome port "corrected" the effect of water on flat ports allowing use of extreme wide-angle lenses.

Notable Underwater Photographers

After equipment had evolved enough to be workable, underwater photographers utilized it to develop as artists. Although it remained essential, it was increasingly apparent that equipment would become secondary to the creative process.

Douglas Faulkner produced underwater photographs that went beyond documentation to the realm of introspective, reflective art. His work with the Rollemarin in the late 1960s combined razor-sharp focus with a sense a composition, texture, and color that remain unique and beautiful to this day. Photographs by Faulkner presented images from then unknown locations like Belau and Papua New Guinea that were visually arresting and evoked a vision of his personal relationship to the ocean.

Many excellent photographers are routinely publishing images that are beyond what photographers could imagine 20 years ago. David Doubilet majored in cinematography at Boston University and has spent his working life as a still photographer at the *National Geographic*. Even in college, he was an underwater photographer, diving with Kenneth R. H. Read and teaching underwater photography at the Cambridge YWCA. His Kodachromes and story telling ability set a modern standard that most serious photographers respect and emulate.

Christopher Newbert is a self-taught, professional photographer who has published widely but most expressively in his own books. These coffee table volumes contain only a fraction of the images he has collected during months of continuous work under water in Hawaii, the Red Sea, the Galapagos, the Solomons, New Guinea, and elsewhere.

Essentials of Underwater Photography

"People who describe the enchanting riot of color in tropical reef fairylands are talking about the environment down to perhaps twenty five feet. Below that, even in sunflooded tropical shallows, one can see only about half the real color values. The sea is a bluing agent."
        Jacques-Yves Cousteau, 1953, <u>The Silent World</u>

How Water Affects Light

Passage through water alters the characteristics of light, compared to its relatively unimpeded travel through air. First and perhaps most important, no water is really clear. Water contains floating particles that disperse, reflect, and absorb light. The final effect is a hazy world lacking contrast, in which light rapidly fades to blue.

The optical densities of air and water differ. Light travels more slowly in water, since it is more dense. Optical density would be unimportant if air and water interfaces did not occur and cause light refraction. Since the human eye evolved to focus in air, not water, we must first look through an airspace inside the diver's mask that refracts light approaching the eye.

Since the speed of light in water (135,000 mi/s) is only about 3/4 of the speed of light in air (186,000 mi/s), the degree of magnification is 1/3. Besides making objects appear closer, magnification by water has important practical effects on lenses focused behind flat ports.

Magnification by water *increases* the effective focal length of macrolenses behind flat ports. For example, a 60mm lens acts as if it were an 80mm lens, a 105mm lens as if it were a 140mm lens, and a 200mm lens as if it were a 266mm lens. Magnification is not a problem with wide-angle lenses housed behind dome ports, because the dome creates a virtual image on which the lens focuses.

The intensity of ambient light is most critical in wide-angle photography. Ambient light decreases rapidly with depth. Particles in water absorb light, turning it into heat energy.

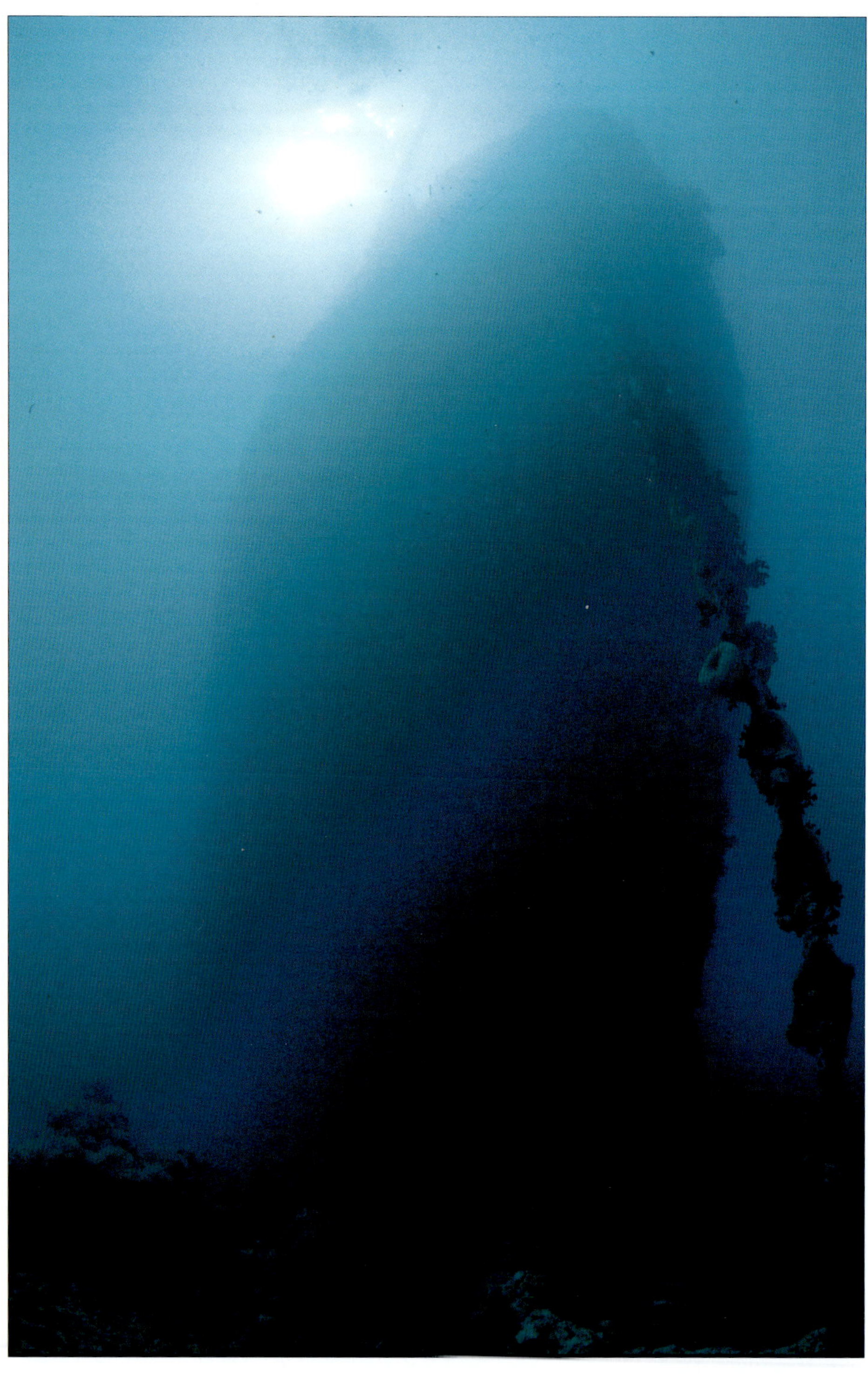

Essentials of Underwater Photography

The effect is more evident where water is more turbid. For example, a 120-fsw dive at noon in New England might require artificial light. A dive to an identical depth in relatively sediment free water, like in the Red Sea, would require no lights and often the sun would be visible from depth. Because of reflection from suspended particles, light is also scattered, making it more diffuse and less intense.

On land and in water, all light has direction. Light in the water seems more diffuse and direction is less apparent when available light is the only source.

The surface of the water also reflects light, so not all sunlight reaching the surface is actually transmitted into the water column. More light is reflected as the sunlight becomes less perpendicular to the surface. Assuming sunlight at noon is neutral in color, sunrise and sunset seem warm (more red) in comparison.

Water also changes the color of light. Besides loss of overall light because of reflection and dispersion, light changes color as it travels deeper. Depending on dissolved materials, water tends to selectively absorb red light resulting in blue. The relative amount of red to blue light decreases with depth. However, not all water is blue. In northern latitudes, water may be a green or brown, and photographs with a blue background (because of film characteristics) would appear false. Selective scattering affects the color of water, as it does the sky. Blue light scatters more than other colors because of its wavelength.

Light in the ocean depends on the sunlight and weather above the surface. Factors determining how much light is present at depth include the time of day and the height of the sun above the ocean.

Opposite page, the wreck of the Thistlegorn in the Red Sea. The wreck was discovered by the Cousteau team in the 1950s and first photographed by L. Marden. The photograph is taken from the bottom (120 fsw) and looks up at the bow. There is an extreme range of exposure values from the bottom to the sun at surface. The wreck appears in silhouette. This exposure was obtained by bracketing all f stops, and choosing the best exposure on the light table. **(Nikon F3; PKL; available light; 16mm lens; 1/60 second at f8)**

Next page, the wreck of the Hilma Hooker in Bonaire. The wreck is shown in silhouette. The ocean appears deep blue because of the Ektachrome film. The exposure was obtained by metering the midwater column. The original image is extremely sharp, because of the water contact optics of the Nikonos lens. **(Nikonos V; Ektachrome 200; available light; 15mm lens; 1/60 second at f5.6)**

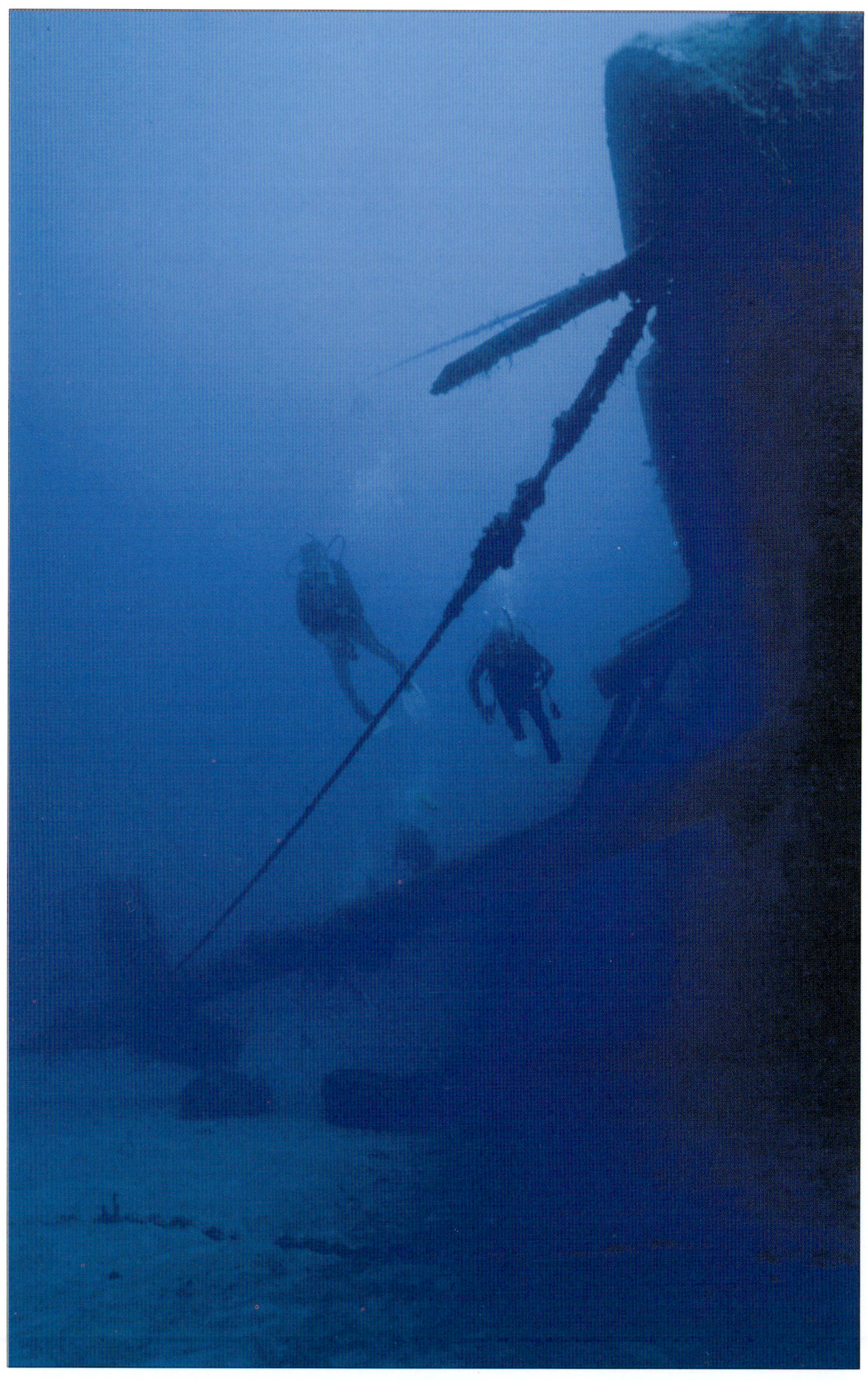

Essentials of Underwater Photography

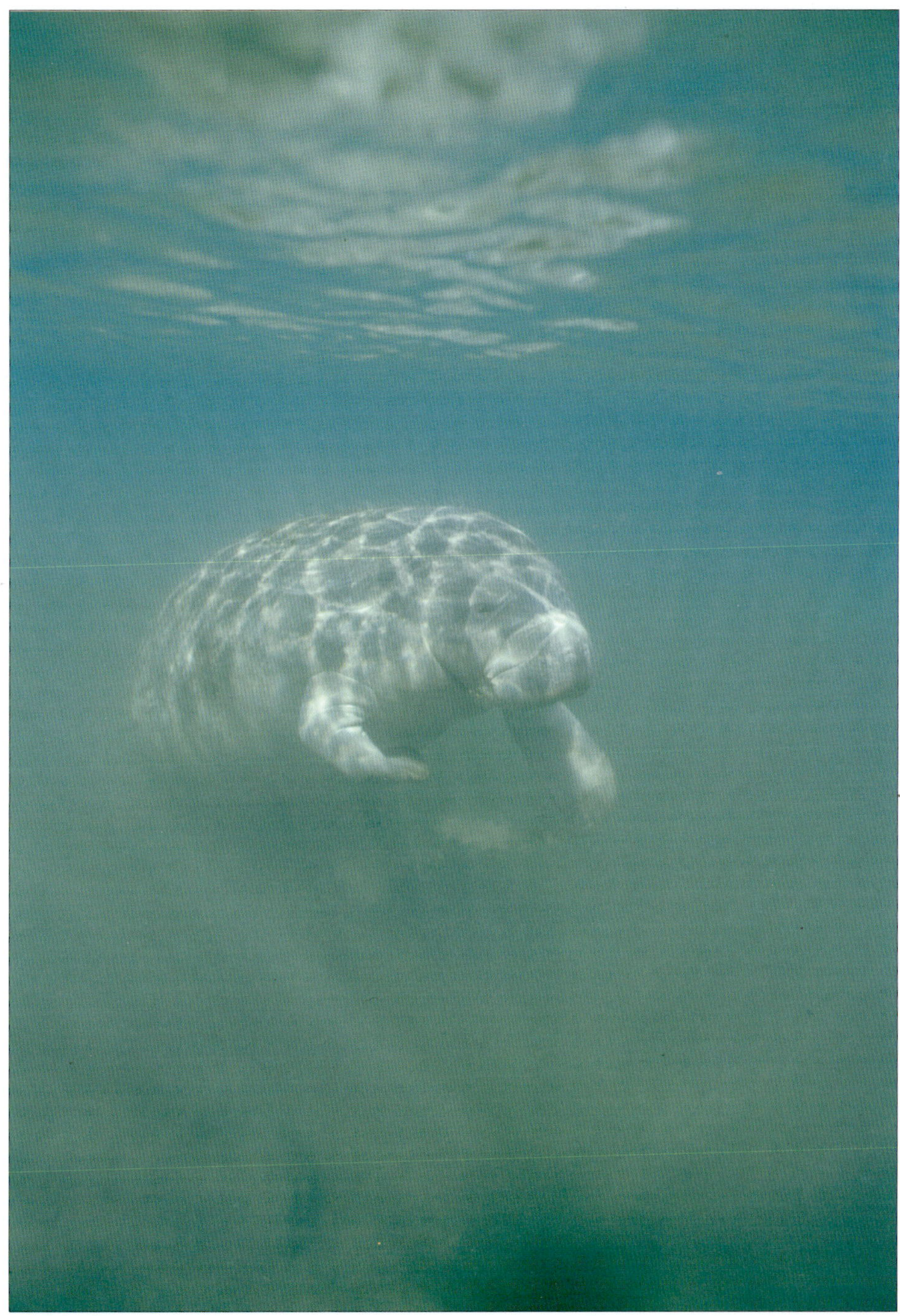

Manatee photographed in Crystal Springs, Florida. The manatee remained still as I floated and I made several available light exposures. The water is shallow and the colors appear warm. Light reflecting in shafts from the bottom emphasized the erect position and vertical composition of the subject. **(Nikon F; Ektachrome 64 (EPR); available light; 28mm lens; 1/60 second at *f*11)**

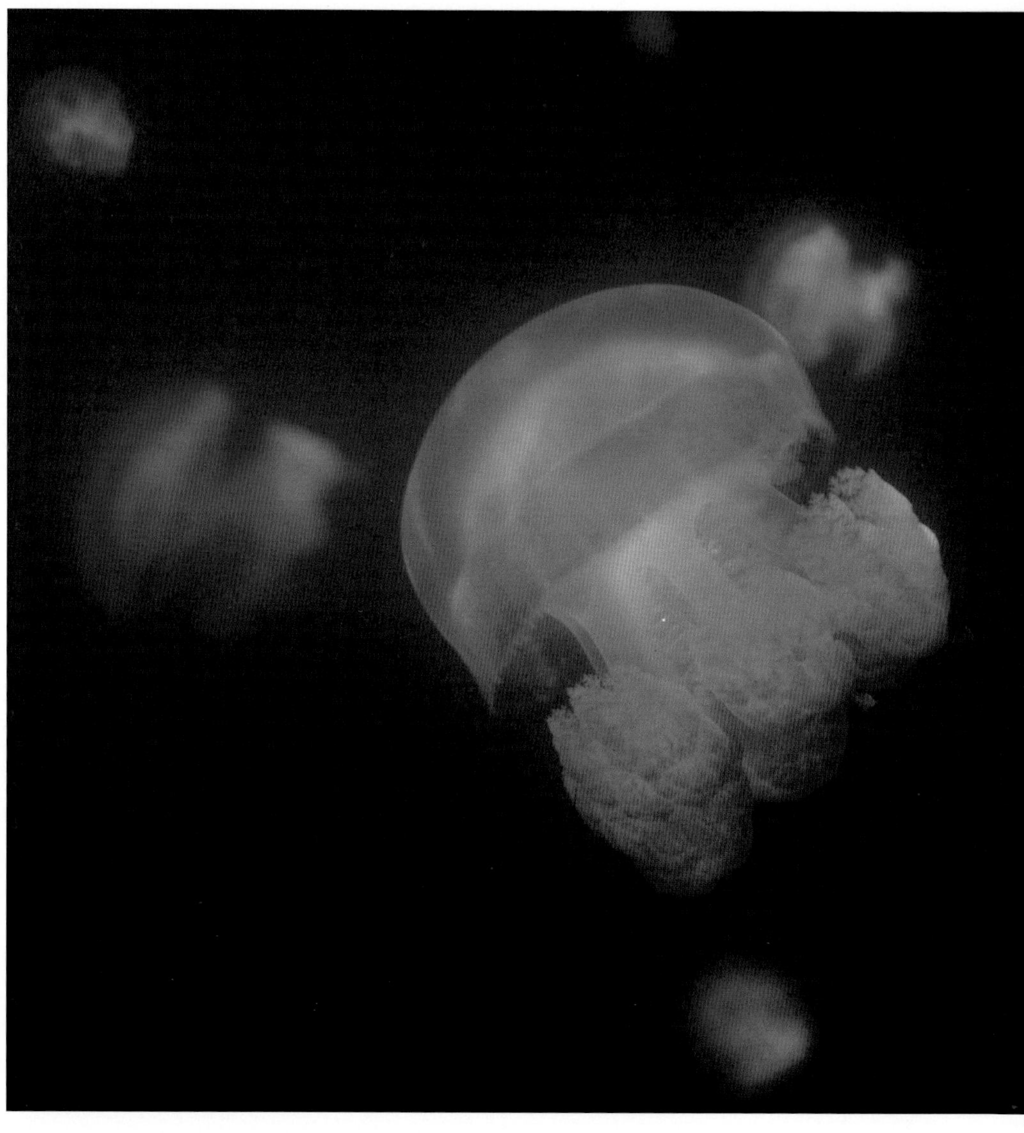

More sunlight reaches deeper during midday when the sun is most vertical, resulting in less reflection from the surface.

On land, photographs made in the early morning or late afternoon
are most interesting because light is horizontal, warmer in color, and
gives greater contrast. Photographing under water at those times is usually not possible, since insufficient light is available.

                    Essentials of Underwater Photography

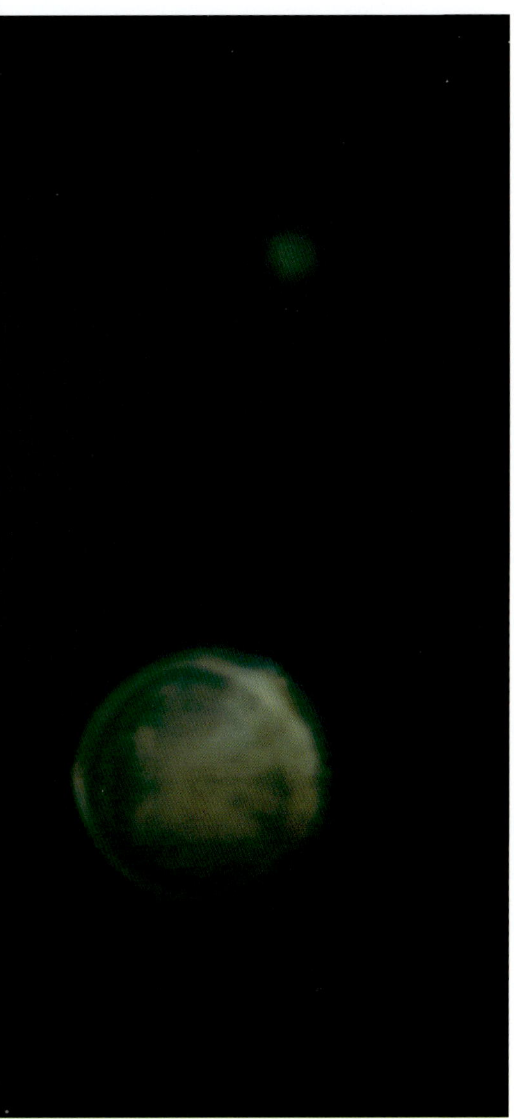

Mastigias jellyfish photographed in Jellyfish Marine Lake (Oreor Island), Republic of Belau. The photograph was taken with available light: The sun was behind and above the jellyfish in the center of the photograph. The correct exposure was obtained by bracketing widely, as I fired the motor drive. The jellyfish captures the light and the background is slightly underexposed. The composition is diagonal with the long axis of the jellyfish placed at about 45° in the frame. **(Nikon F3; Kodachrome 64 (PKR); available light; 55mm Micro Nikkor lens; 1/60 second at f5.6)**

Light Meters

Light meters measure light from surfaces (*reflected light*) or light falling on the meter itself (*incident light*). Light meters work by converting light directly to electrical current (selenium cells) or by sensing a change in electrical resistance due to light falling on a sensor (cadmium sulfide). Most light meters in camera bodies use cadmium sulfide sensors. Although they are becoming difficult to obtain, independent light meters are a great advantage in underwater photography. One product, the reliable and accurate Sekonic Marine Meter, has served underwater photographers well for many years.

Light meters are simple analog computers that one can program with film speed (i.e., its sensitivity to light) and shutter speed. The light meter then predicts the aperture required for that combination of film and shutter speed based on available light. The prediction is, at best, an approximation. The result usually is accurate because film has such a wide exposure latitude (margin of error). Even with a light meter, bracketing is necessary for technically and artistically acceptable exposures.

Light meters differ in the angle of view the sensor accepts. They may be "weighted" to favor the measurement from one part (e.g., center or bottom) of the field of view. The Sekonic Marine Meter has a narrow angle of acceptance (<15°) so that one can accurately target a point in the water column. This allows the photographer to aim the meter precisely relative to the sun.

Most simple selenium meters have a much wider angle of acceptance. They produce an average exposure reading, which may not accurately give the desired background exposure, thus emphasizing the need to bracket exposures.

The Nikonos V meter is an internal cadmium sulfide sensor. It is "bottom weighted," meaning it gets most exposure information from the bottom 1/3 of the frame. Such bottom weighting tends to overexpose the middle and upper parts of the water column. Using an external, independent light meter with a narrow acceptance field overcomes this problem.

Meters to measure incident light are rarely used under water, although some housings for meters are available. These frequently also function as a flash meter, and are useful for testing function of strobes. Most often flash/incident meters cannot be used to find flash exposure under water, because the situation is too dynamic. Finding proper flash exposure for use under water is described in Chapter 6.

Light meters estimate film speed based on reflectance values of average objects in typical lighting conditions. Objects that are not of "average" reflectance may give incorrect light meter readings leading to wrong exposures. Light meters were designed to give accurate readings from grey surfaces that reflect 18% of incident light. Surfaces that are highly reflective, e.g., bright white sand, will appear underexposed because more than 18% of the light is reflected. If less than 18% of light is reflected (e.g., from a black wall) the resulting photograph will appear overexposed. The photographer must correct the exposure in a way that may seem backwards at first. If the white sand appears bright, increase the exposure (above the meter reading) by opening the aperture. If the surface appears too dark, decrease the exposure by closing the aperture.

Varying reflectance does not tend to be a problem in the water. Particles throughout the water scatter light, rather than reflect it, and so extremes affect light meter readings less. No light meter is completely accurate. The photographer must always bracket exposure based on the light meter reading, which is only an approximate indication based on assumptions of averages.

Light meters are most helpful in correct exposure of the blue water background. A narrow angle of acceptance is useful, as in the previously described Sekonic Marine Meter. Correct exposure of the blue water background is somewhat arbitrary and depends on personal preference. Usually, acceptable exposure will be found in midwater (with the photographer aiming the meter straight ahead). The meter should point about 45-60° away from the sun. Otherwise, the meter will show an exposure for the sun itself and underexpose the water column. Deviation from a typical background blue may also be acceptable. Overexposure can lighten the shade of blue and underexposure can increase contrast. "Correct" exposure for the blue water background is, within limits, both subjective and arbitrary.

Filters

Filters selectively eliminate parts of the visible spectrum by absorbing specific wavelengths. Total light reaching the film is *decreased* and the exposure must be *increased* to compensate. Filters may decrease the light reaching the film by two or more f stops. Filters are used to increase contrast in black and white photography and to change the color of light in color photography. Yellow filters (e.g., K-2) increase contrast of black and white film. Red filters (CR20 or CCR30) are sometimes used to eliminate the imbalance between red and blue light at depth. This corrects the bluish cast of color film exposed with available light. Warm colors produced by incorporating a red filter may look artificial, especially immediately below the surface where plenty of red light is already present.

Conclusions

Successful use of available light means choosing an appropriate **combination** of aperture and shutter speed. Overall, midrange apertures (e.g., $f5.6$ - $f11$) give the best image quality, which is always a compromise between necessary depth of field, sharpness, and flare.

Filters Commonly Used for Color Photography

Filter	ƒ Stop Increase	Effect	Application	Film
UV	none	Eliminates haze and blue cast	Altitude, deserts, lens protection	Color or black and white
Skylight	none	Slight shift to warmer spectrum	General, lens protection	Color or black and white
Polarizing	~1-1.5	Darkens sky, removes glare and reflections	Daylight	Color or black and white
80A	~2	Cooler spectrum	Tungsten light	Daylight color
85B	~2/3	Warmer spectrum	Daylight	Tungsten color
FLD	~1	Magenta shift	Fluorescent light	Daylight color
CCR10R-50R	0-2	Red shift	Under water	Daylight color

Smaller apertures give greater depth of field, i.e., a greater acceptable zone of focus. The sharpest apertures usually occur about two f stops below the largest aperture (e.g., $f5.6$ on an $f2.8$ lens).

Extremely small apertures distort light by diffraction (distortion) of light passing near the edges of the iris and can actually decrease sharpness. Very large apertures reduce effective depth of field and can introduce aberrant colors (chromatic distortion) in the light that eventually hits the film. Understanding correct aperture and shutter speed choice in available light photography is critical in using combination lighting for wide-angle, strobe-filled photography, as further described in Chapter 6.

CHAPTER 3

CAMERAS AND THEIR FUNCTIONS

- Camera
- Shutter
- Aperture

"Basically all cameras are very much alike, whether they cost $4.95 or $495, and three varying elements account for the wide variance in price — lens, shutter, and viewfinder."
E.R. Cross, 1954,
<u>Underwater Photography and Television</u>

Cameras

Cameras contain and advance film, while controlling the amount and form of light. Other functions may be important or useful in some situations, but they are not essential to the creation of an image. Modern cameras used under water are designed so that focusing and composition take place through a single, primary lens. Single lens reflex cameras (SLRs) permit use of many interchangeable lenses. A focal plane shutter and variable iris control the amount of light striking the film. A lens gathers and focuses light on the viewing screen and film. Most 35mm SLR cameras used under water contain a motor-driven winder that allows the photographer to aim, compose, follow action, and shoot — all while keeping the eye on the viewfinder.

The Nikonos V camera is an exception. It has a viewfinder useful only for aiming; focusing is done by guessing or measuring camera to subject distance (e.g., with framers). The camera body holds a canister of 35mm film that advances manually from frame to frame.

Most underwater photographs are taken with 35mm cameras because of their versatility and the variety of interchangeable lenses. Far fewer medium format SLR cameras are available, but some have been housed (e.g., the Hasselblad) and these can produce large, spectacular transparencies. The most widely available formats are 6x6 cm and 6x7 cm, but expense and size have limited their use, even among professional underwater photographers. This book concentrates on 35mm equipment because that format comprises over 95% of equipment in use today.

Shutter

The shutter controls how much light reaches the film by controlling the time that light falls on the film. Shutter speeds are described as fractions of seconds, usually ranging from 1/30 to 1/500 second. These are frequently written as "30," "60," "125," and so on. Slower and faster speeds are rarely used under water. Shutter speeds usually differ by a doubling factor (e.g., 1/30, 1/60, 1/125, 1/250...) corresponding to the *f* stop scale.

Most shutters in SLR cameras are focal planes that synchronize with the strobe in the 1/30 to 1/250 second range. Curtains that form the shutter partially or completely (i.e., at strobe synch speeds) separate to expose the film to light. When the shutter curtain fully separates, the camera is synchronized with the strobe. When the shutter only partially opens, a slit of light sweeps across the film plane and strobe synchronization cannot occur.

Aperture

The diameter of the lens limits the total amount of light that passes through the lens to reach the film. The light is further controlled by an iris in the lens that controls the aperture opening or *f* stop.

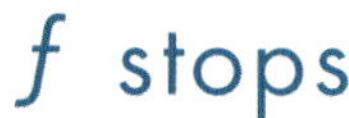

f stops

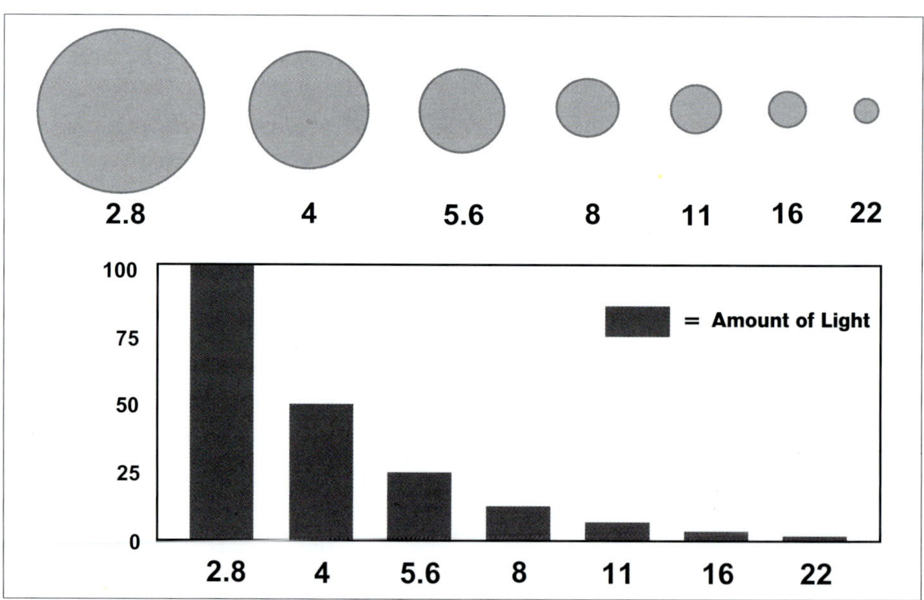

Essentials of Underwater Photography

The "*f* stop" is defined as the focal length of the lens divided by the diameter of the aperture, so a 50 mm focal length lens with the iris aperture of 4.5 mm diameter is at $f11$ (50 mm ÷ 4.5 mm = 11). The *f* stops shown on the barrel usually differ by a factor of 2; each increase in *f* stop allows 1/2 the light of the previous (i.e., smaller number) stop and 2x the light of the next *f* stop (i.e., larger number). The amount of light at $f3.5$ = 2 x $f4.5$ = 2 x $f5.6$ = 2 x $f8$ = 2 x $f11$= 2 x $f16$ = 2 x $f22$, and so on. An *f* stop table follows:

f stop table in 0.1 *f* stop units

f	.1	.2	.3	.4	.5	.6	.7	.8	.9
1.4	1.5	1.5	1.6	1.7	1.7	1.8	1.8	1.9	1.9
2	2.1	2.2	2.3	2.4	2.4	2.5	2.6	2.7	2.8
2.8	2.9	3.1	3.2	3.3	3.4	3.5	3.7	3.8	3.9
4	4.2	4.4	4.6	4.7	4.9	5.1	5.2	5.4	5.5
5.6	5.9	6.1	6.4	6.6	6.9	7.1	7.3	7.5	7.7
8	8.4	8.8	9.1	9.5	9.8	10.1	10.4	10.7	11.0
11	11.5	12	12.5	13.0	13.5	13.9	14.3	14.8	15.2
16	16.8	17.5	18.2	18.9	19.6	20.2	20.9	21.5	22.1
22	23.1	24.1	25.1	26	26.9	27.8	28.7	29.5	30.3

Opposite page, diagram showing *f* stops and relative area through which light passes. As the *f* stop number increases, the size of the opening decreases. The amount of light passing through each opening decreases by 1/2 as the *f* stop number increases (the area increases by 1/2).

If the lens zooms (increases in length) to change focal length, the effective f stop changes as well. This "bellows effect" occurred with earlier versions of the Micro Nikkor lens. At longer focal lengths, the seemingly smaller f stop allows less light to pass, so the lens appears to have a smaller opening and a larger f number. While the lens might indicate $f11$, only as much light as if it were at $f22$ may actually pass through. Automated cameras correct for the bellows effect and show the effective f stop on an LED readout. The effect has little importance for setting exposure, if TTL systems are used.

COMPOSITION

"In essence you must stalk the fish and then try to find a place 'to land,' to place yourself in order to make an intimate photograph of the creature. 'Intimate' is the most accurate description of a successful photograph. The image of the eye of the fish, the shark or the seal must penetrate through the sea, the camera lens, on to a piece of film and finally into the viewer's eye."

David Doubilet, 1988, <u>The Manual of Underwater Photography</u> (H. deCouet and A. Green, aus.)

Definition

Beyond repeating the dictionary, composition is hard to define. The notion refers to how objects (shapes and forms) arrange themselves in a field of vision. But composition also applies to one's reaction to that placement. "Good" composition is an arbitrary idea that suggests a harmonious distribution of forms and color in space. We experience composition from a point of view that can be either objective or subjective. Objective changes in a point of view reflect physical movement of the eye or change in the field of vision. Subjective changes in point of view imply new perceptions, which may not require movement at all — only a new way of seeing.

Composition has several intrinsic elements. Most photographs, except perhaps for seascapes, have a primary subject (e.g., a nudibranch) that creates a focal point for the photograph. Placement of the primary subject largely defines the photographic composition. The eye "moves" through a photograph, and thus requires an entrance path and an exit that appear natural. Elements of composition should balance. Apparently unnatural or uncomfortable weighting or distribution of mass in the scene should be avoided.

Balance suggests symmetry and harmonious placement of shapes (mass) in the frame. Balance means that compositions have a center of gravity, which need not be in the center of the frame. The rule of 1/3's or the 5/8's rule should guide its

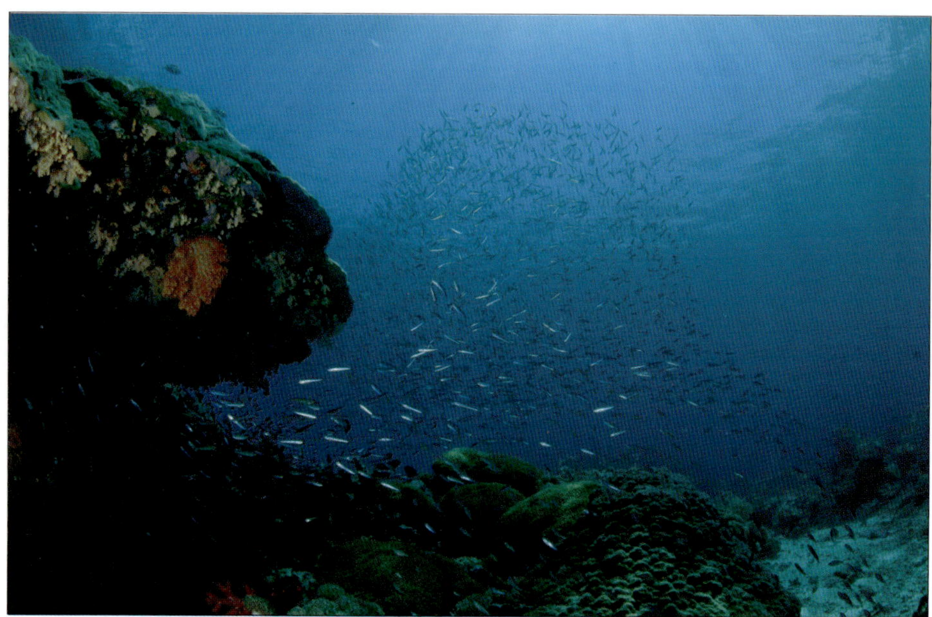

Silversides (baitfish) at Anuha in the Solomon Islands. The fish arrange themselves in a pyramid between my camera and the sun. The group is framed by part of the reef. The photograph is made dramatic by the vertical beams of light seen coming from the surface. **(Nikon F3; Lumiere 100 (LPZ); 16mm lens; available light with strobe fill in; two Sea and Sea YS-200 strobes; 1/60 second at ƒ11)**

placement, so that the eye is guided away from the center of the frame. The point of interest should not be centered, but should be balanced, by a less well defined point or by negative space.

The final element of composition, the photograph's mood, is less objective and harder to define. Mood implies an overall impression created by the photograph and the feelings it evokes in the viewer.

Practical Aspects

Position of the camera and the photographer is critically important in creating the composition. Physical movement of the camera can change the arrangement of forms, shapes, and space in the frame and alter the composition. Unlike land-based photographers, underwater photographers have the unique ability to move in three dimensions. Composition implies a viewer's location compared with the subject. Putting larger objects in front and smaller objects in the rear provides perspective. Perspective (the angle of view) can be made to seem shorter in macrotelephoto shots or exaggerated in extreme wide-angles. Perspective can be "forced" by placing objects close to the dome port, or by using upward camera angles.

Essentials of Underwater Photography

A photographer should bracket composition in addition to exposure and focus. Sometimes, the best composition can be judged only when viewing a series of slides that differ slightly from each other on the light table.

Standard Approaches

Accepted rules, which can and occasionally should be broken, govern composition. Division of the frame horizontally or vertically into thirds (the "rule of thirds") is a traditional technique for harmonious, off center placement of the primary subject. In this approach the frame is divided as follows:

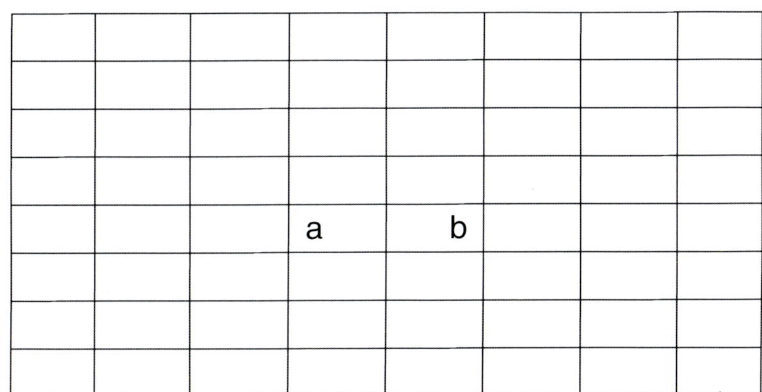

The points at which the primary subject might be placed are shown by **a** or **b**. Placement of a fish's eye at **a** or **b** will have more visual impact than placing it in the center of the frame. Exceptions to this rule can create pleasing compositions, so it is not rigid. A photographer can also move the point of sharpest focus to create a more interesting composition than the typical (autofocus) approach in which only the exact center of the frame is sharply focused.

The rule of 5/8's is another variant of the rule of 1/3's. The frame is divided into 1/8's instead of 1/3's. For example:

This moves the point of interest (**a** or **b**) closer to the center of the frame. You could also draw a 3 x 3 or 8 x 8 grid on the focusing screen as a reminder.

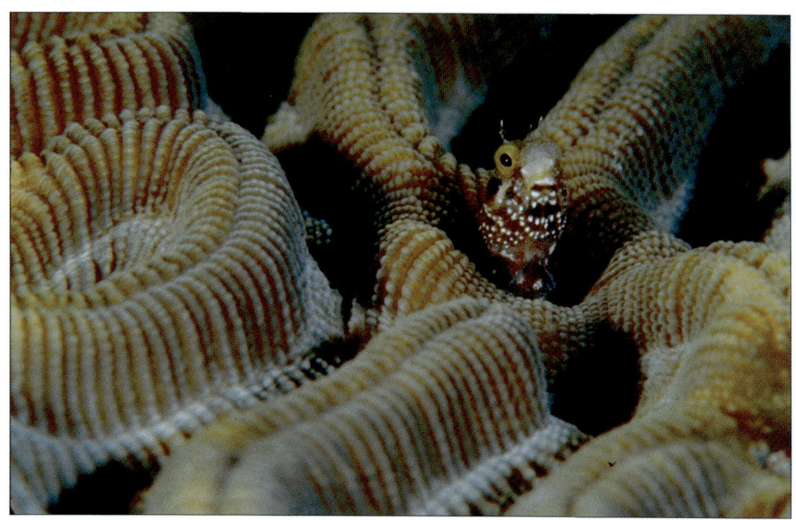

A goby emerging from a piece of brain coral. Note the texture of the coral that is accented by the side lighting. The goby (the point of interest) is placed off center (the rule of $\frac{1}{3}$'s) and yet remains in sharp focus. **(Nikon F3; LPZ 100 film, 105mm lens; Nikonos SB-105 and SB-103 strobes; 1/60 second at ƒ11)**

Essentials of Underwater Photography

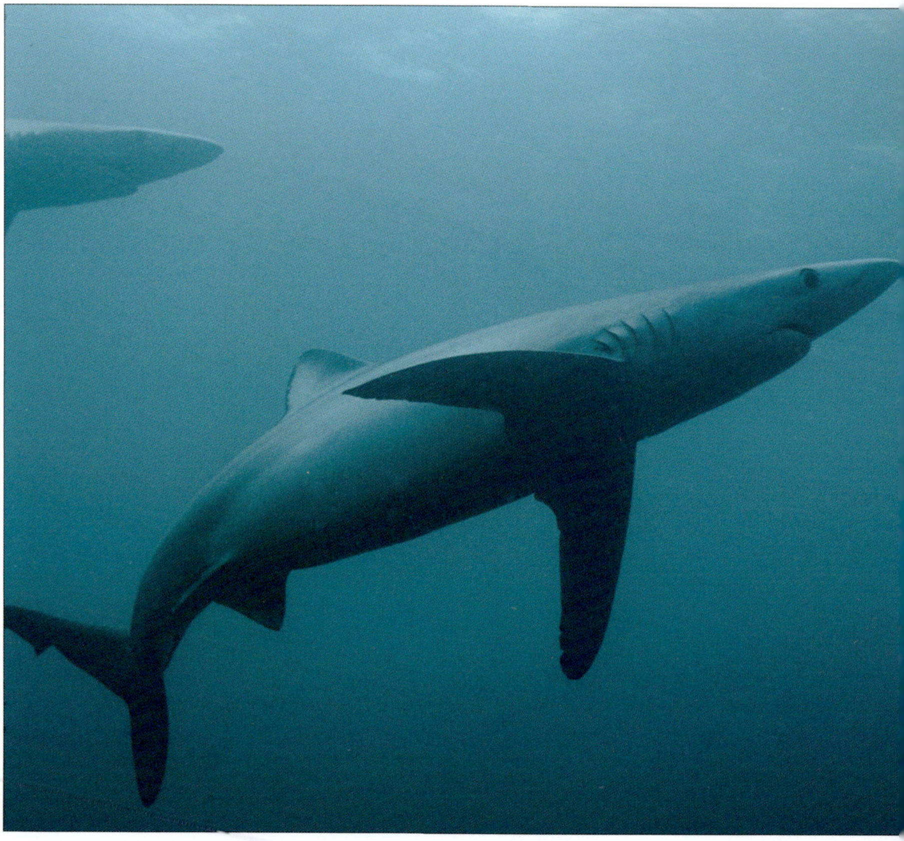

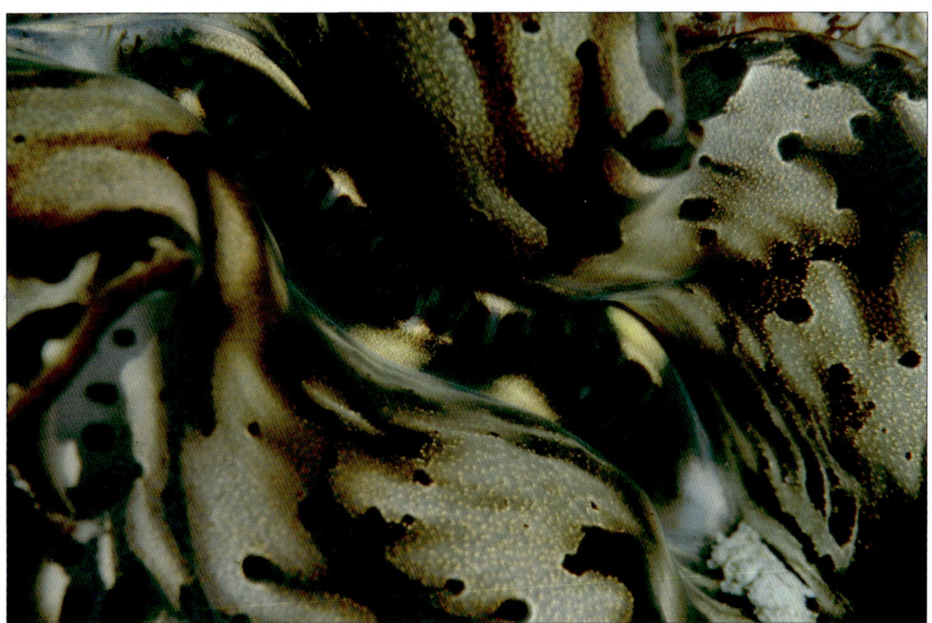

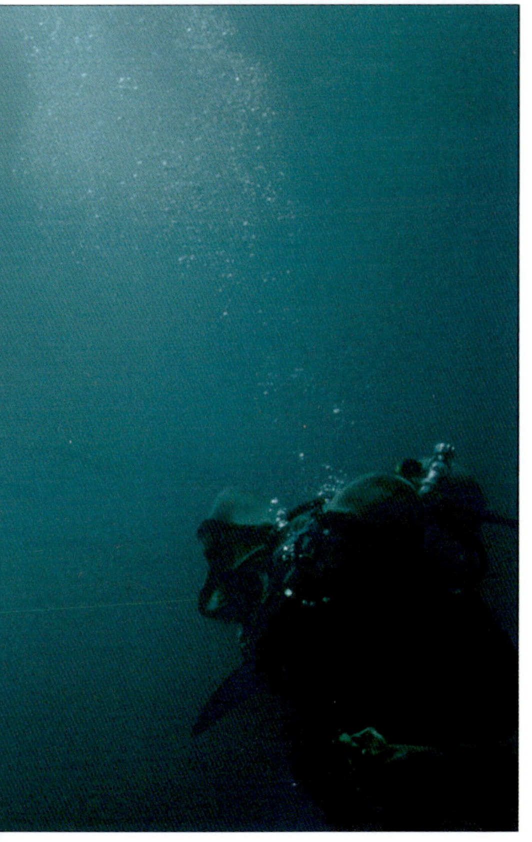

Above, Tridachna clam mantle. The most striking aspect of the composition is the gentle s-curve formed by the orifice of the mantle. The gold in the flesh of the mantle creates highlights. The image is sharp and warm because of the Kodachrome 25 film used. **(Nikon F3; PKM film; 105mm lens; Nikonos SB-105 and SB-103 strobes; 1/60 second at ƒ11)**

A blue shark photographed in the open ocean emphasizes the diagonal and curved lines important in composition. The angle is upward, and the exposure was taken from a meter reading of the blue water. **(Nikon F3; Kodachrome 200; 17mm lens; 1/60 at ƒ8)**

Lines and Curves

Diagonal lines create more visual interest and suggest greater movement than straight lines or 90° angles. Lines (e.g., the long axis of a fish) that run parallel to the edge of the frame do not stimulate interest in the composition. Straight lines and square corners should also be avoided. Curves occupy space in a way that implies graceful movement. More typically, gentle S-curves traverse the frame diagonally. Opposing curves may also create forms that imply movement, but also suggest balance.

Space

Composition makes space important, since objects must be arranged in space. Light passes through space to illuminate an object, and the eye must travel through space to find the point of interest. Composition uses space to define and contain important elements of an image. Space can be full (positive) or empty (negative). A subject, usually one that draws the eye, makes the positive space. Directional light can emphasize the positive space by directing the eye to this space. Light will direct the eye to the positive space by its direction.

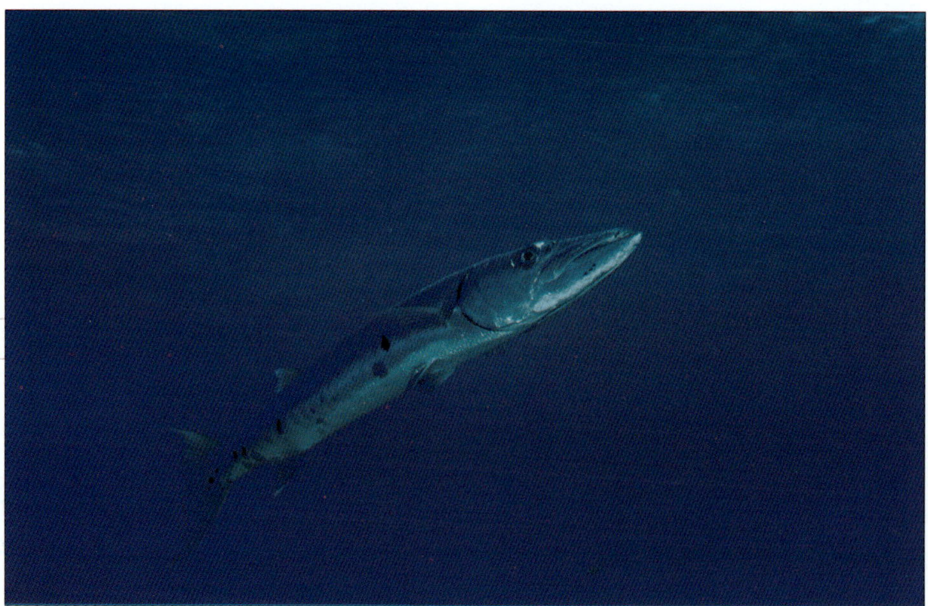

Barracuda from the same perspective (below and angled) as the shark on page 24. The exposure was determined by the highly reflective scales, so the water is deep blue. **(Nikon F; Kodachrome 64; 20mm lens; Honeywell 770 Strobonar on full manual; 1/60 second at ƒ16)**

Essentials of Underwater Photography

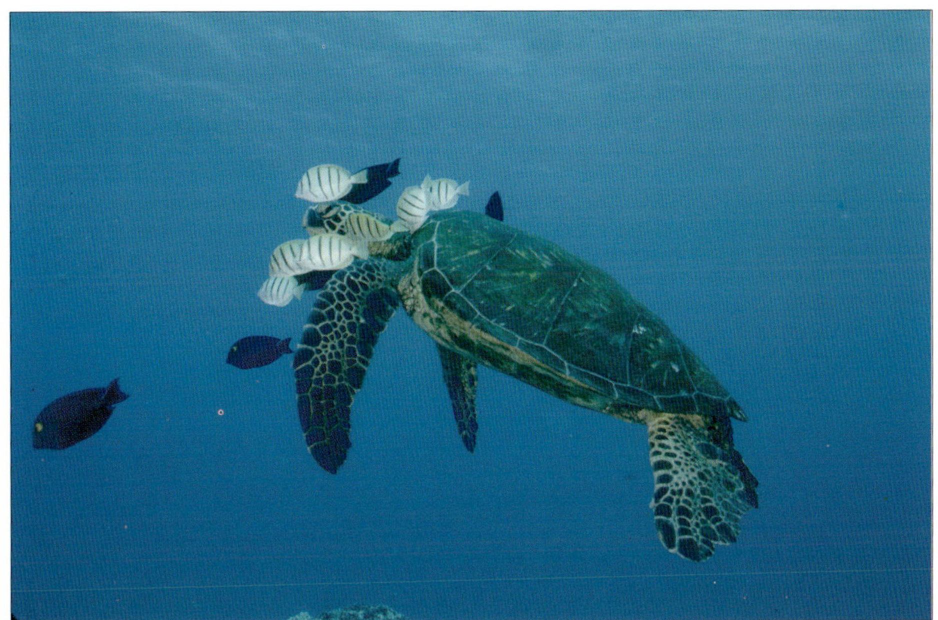

A green turtle suspended over a cleaning station shot with available light and fill-in flash. As in the previous examples, the composition is diagonal on a corner-to-corner line. The exposure was set by a meter reading of the blue water. Correct strobe exposure was then found by "bracketing" strobe power (full or half; with or without diffusers). **(Nikon F3; PKR; available light with fill-in strobe; 28mm lens; two Sea and Sea YS-200 strobes on 1/2 power; 1/60 second at ƒ5.6)**

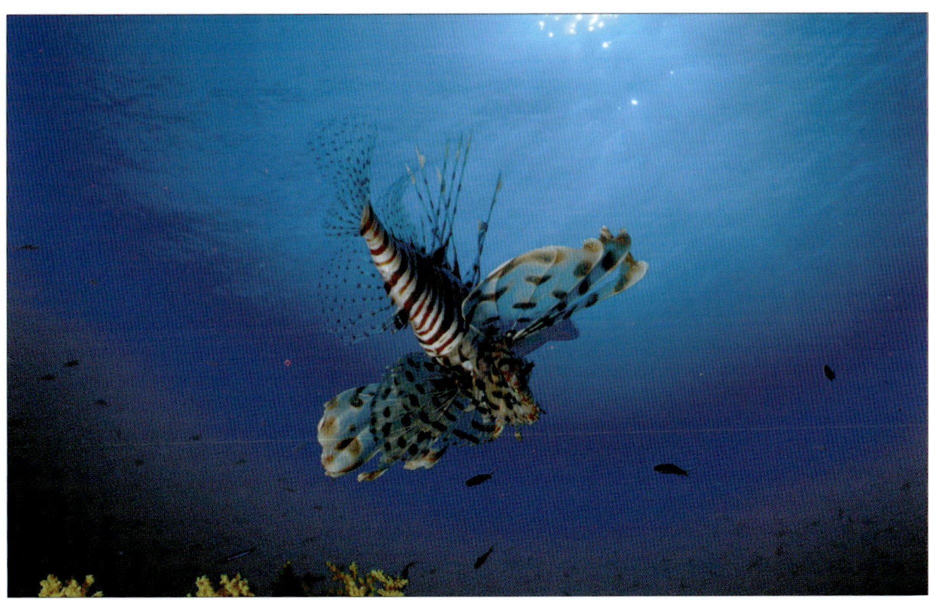

Lionfish photographed from below, as it swam over a reef in the Red Sea. Again, as in the previous examples, the composition is diagonal but the subject is set off from the center of the frame. The exposure balanced sunlight and strobe illumination of the fish's underside. **(Nikon F3; LPZ 100; available light with fill-in strobe; 28mm lens; two Sea and Sea YS-200 strobes on 1/2 power; 1/60 second at ƒ11)**

Negative space can be more important than positive space because it contains and surrounds subjects of interest. Ideal negative space would be uncluttered and not distracting. Tiny, white flecks due to particles in the water (called backscatter) frequently occur in the negative space of strobe-lighted compositions. Minimizing backscatter (see Chapter 6) is an important part of making negative space which is appealing. Negative space may imply darkness and shadow, but negative space can also be lighted. It usually has no focal point and could be the unfocused part of an image. Negative space has no focal points and should present a non-distracting background for the composition.

Enhancing Composition

An implied story enhances composition. Photographs of animals may show a behavior. Action that is self explanatory makes a story in a single photograph. Always isolate the subject in negative space, imply motion, and capture light and gesture.

CHAPTER 5

FILMS

- Introduction

- Choosing Films Based on Application

- Types of Films Based on Processing

- Storing and Handling Films

"To find the film that best suits your technique, try them all. Choose the one you find the most suitable and use it exclusively until you become completely familiar with its characteristics. Deviate from it only when you need to."
Albert Moldvay, 1981,
National Geographic Photographer's Field Guide

Introduction

The choice of film for underwater photography depends on the goals of the photographer and on the general water conditions. The film used to photograph a 1 cm nudibranch using full strobe lighting will, more than likely, not be the same chosen for large, rapidly moving objects like dolphins or sharks in available light.

All choices in photography involve compromise. Fast films (ISO 200 or more) have more grain and higher contrast than slow films (ISO 64 or less). Color rendition by high speed films may be less accurate, and some films differentiate black from grey better than others. The many types of films available and the need to become completely familiar with a few means that the photographer should test several films extensively. Those found most useful to macro, close-up, blue water wide-angle, and reef scenics should be chosen and their characteristics noted.

Shoot enough test rolls to become completely familiar with:

- Color rendition — use a MacBeth color checker to test the response of the film to over- or underexposure

- Effects of sunlight and strobe on the film's color rendition

- Response of color, contrast, and grain to pushing (increasing ISO) or pulling (decreasing ISO) during development

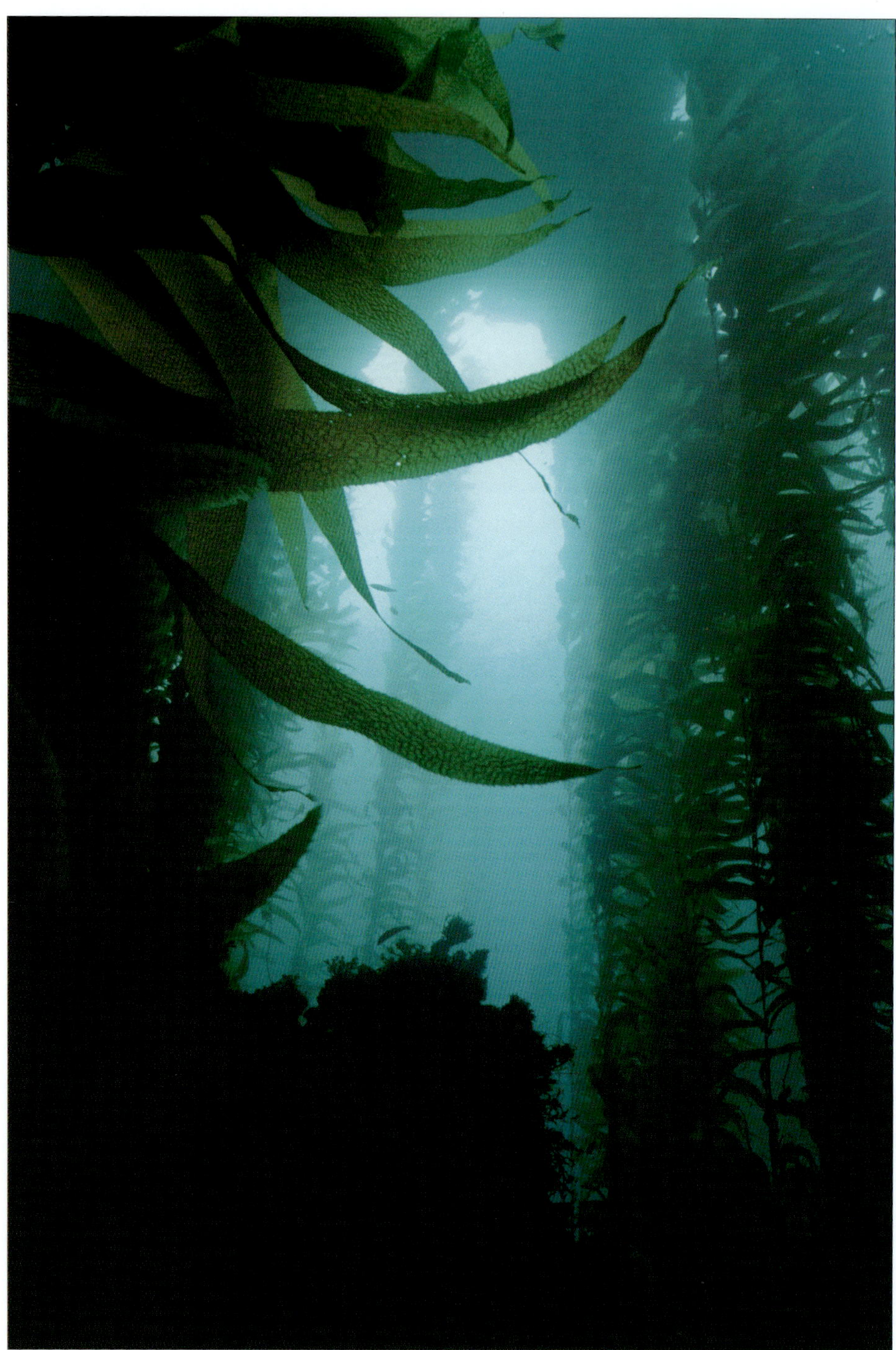

A kelp forest photographed with available light. The perspective is up-looking. Empty space is framed by the kelp itself, appearing almost in silhouette. The film chosen is ideal for such available light shooting: Kodachrome 200. **(Nikonos V; PKL; 20mm lens; available light; 1/60 second at ƒ11)**

Essentials of Underwater Photography

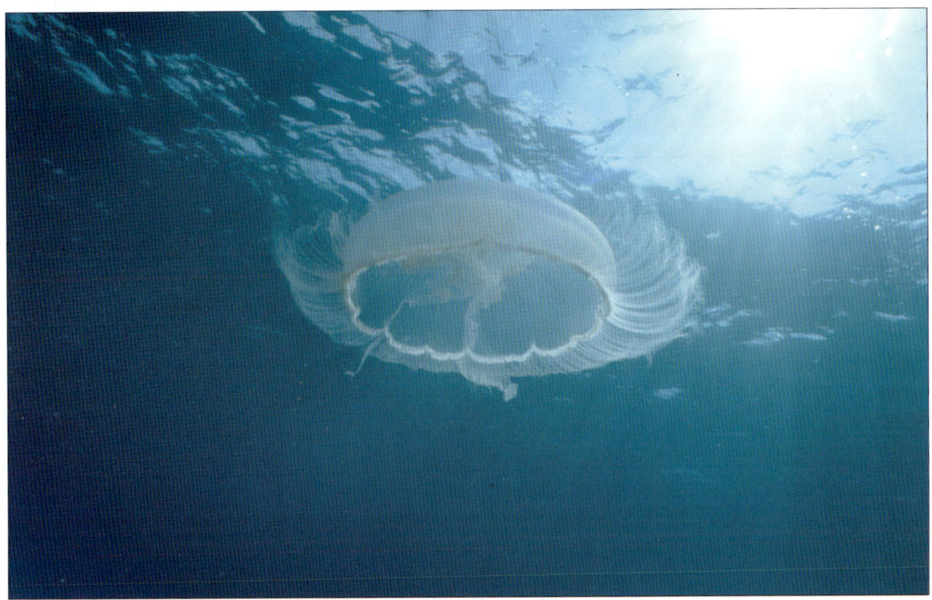

Moon jellyfish (*Aurelia* sp.) photographed in "silhouette." The photograph was made near the surface with available light. No meter reading was accurate, so this exposure was chosen from a wide range of bracketed shots. **(Nikon F; EPR; 28mm lens; available light; 1/60 second at *f* 16)**

Choosing Film Based on Application

The choice of one film (out of hundreds available) becomes much easier if the photographer defines what he/she needs. The best way is to choose a goal and understand the conditions in which this will be accomplished.

Wide-angle lenses and available light or fill in strobe (with mainly available light) are commonly used to photograph fish, turtles, or marine mammals in the open ocean. These conditions (available light, rapidly moving subjects) often require a medium speed (ISO 100) or fast (ISO 200 or more) film. Lower speed films (ISO 64 or less) may also be used for this kind of photography, when ambient light is strong or strobe fill is used on near subjects.

The desired effect (based on previsualization) is accomplished through a choice of film based on knowledge of its characteristics. A common example is that E-6 films, especially Ektachromes, favor blues and make the ocean background appear vividly (sometimes fake) blue, even if the water is green or brown. This may seem attractive, but it can also appear artificial. In contrast, Kodachrome 200 (PKL) film accurately reproduces the ocean background (in reality soft blue or green). PKL is grainy but sharp around the edges. It is relatively high in contrast.

These characteristics make it useful for available light photographs in blue water. Medium speed E-6 processed films (Kodak Ektachromes, Fuji Provia) are also used for this application. This is especially true in clear, tropical waters where the water really is blue.

Other considerations influence the choice of film in macro or close-up photography. Strobe light determines the exposure and color rendition in these photographs, because strobes provide all light needed to make the exposure. Color saturation and impact (rather than accurate color rendition) are desirable characteristics. Because enlargement and projection of macro and close-up photographs is important, fine grain is needed. For these reasons, Fuji Velvia and Kodachrome (25 and 64) have long been films of choice for macrophotography.

Velvia is a highly saturated (deep colors), sharp, and contrasty film, which has become standard for macro and close-up photography. Velvia creates colors like those in print advertising: bright, saturated, and often appearing too "real." Kodachrome 25 (PKM) and 64 (PKR) have been considered the standards for macro and close-up photography. Kodachrome 25 has the finest grain available and is the standard for comparison. Kodachrome 64 is slightly (but barely) less sharp and less warm. It remains an excellent choice for macro and close-up photography.

Decorator crab on a red sponge. The redness of the sponge emphasizes the deeply saturated colors of the Velvia film. The contrast is high and the resolution is excellent. **(Nikon F3; Velvia; 55mm lens; Nikonos SB-105 and SB-103 strobes; 1/60 second at *f*16)**

Types of Film Based on Processing

Films are classified in one of two groups based on processing techniques. Kodachrome films require complicated processing by dedicated laboratories, sometimes franchised by Kodak. Kodachrome films do not contain organic coupling dyes; so chemicals have to be added during processing to match the

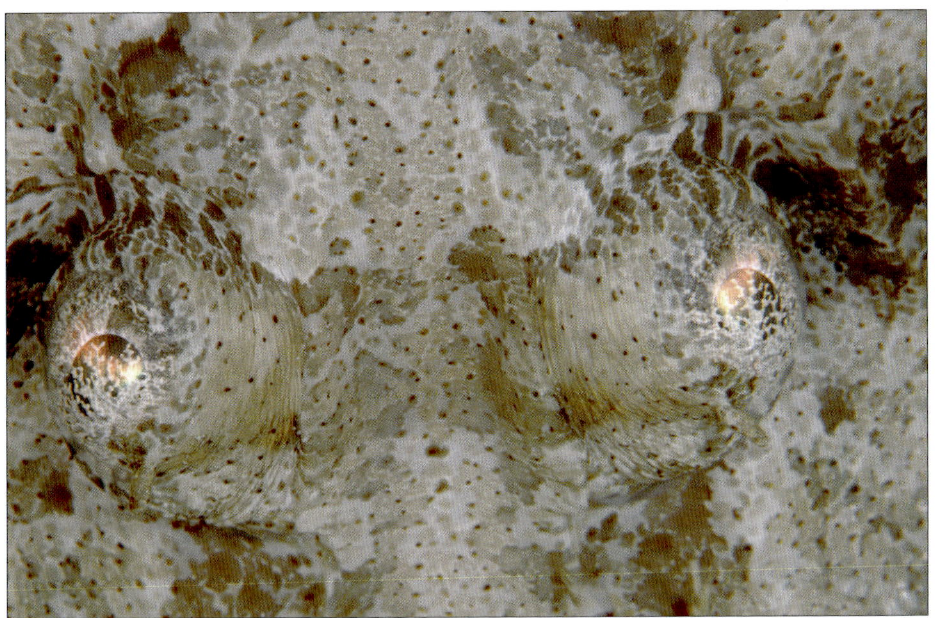

Crocodile fish detail. The photograph was made in the Red Sea on Kodachrome 25 film, which is essentially grain-free and warm. Detail is visible in the skin and strobe light reflected from the eyes of the fish shows the warmth of the film. The contrast is good and the resolution is exceptional. **(Nikon F3; PKM; 105mm Micro Nikkor lens; Nikonos SB-105 and SB-103 strobes; 1/60 second at ƒ8)**

color image. The K14 process is complicated and requires shipment of film (usually a relatively convenient but slow process) and return by mail. Specialized laboratories can push or pull Kodachrome's ISO speed. Pushing is particularly useful for K200, which can be pushed at least one full ƒ stop to provide a warm, saturated high speed film for use in open water.

Kodachrome 25 is a very warm and slow color film that has been the photographic standard since its introduction in the 1930s. The film is sharp and has an extremely fine grain and high resolution. K25 permits projection on large screens and easily enlarges to 16" x 20" and larger. The excellent color stability of K25 is an added advantage. Kodachrome slides can be stored for many years without detectable loss of color.

K64 is similar to K25 in its fine grain and resolution. K64 may produce less saturated greens and reds than some popular E-6 film. When exposed at ISO 80, the saturation and contrast of K64 increases notably. K64 produces fully saturated blacks (more than most E-6 films) and, as a result, is favored for available light shots that silhouette fish, sharks, or mammals against the sunlit blue sea. It withstands underexposure much better than overexposure. Like all slide films, Kodachrome should be exposed for the brightest, whitest parts of the subject.

Kodachrome 200 (PKL) is a warm, sharp, high speed slide film that is useful for shooting pelagic fish, sharks, and mammals in open water. Color rendition is warm and produces soft, powdery blue or light green water that accurately reflects color. Despite its obviously visible grain, the film has excellent edge sharpness and makes fine enlargements. The high speed makes it ideal for fast-moving subjects in open water. Laboratories able to process Kodachrome can push the film by one or more *f* stops to create a fast film ideal for rapidly moving objects in low light.

Despite traditional advantages such as grain size, sharpness, accuracy of color rendition, and archival (storage) properties, Kodachrome films have become less popular than E-6 films (originally Ektachrome, but now including Fuji and Agfa films). Modern E-6 films are easy to process with resulting vivid, high contrast images. One advantage of E-6 film is the convenience with which it can be processed and checked for correct exposure and camera function. Disadvantages of E-6 processing include the variability of quality in the field (for example, impure water results in spotting and streaking) resulting from a lack of temperature and time standardization.

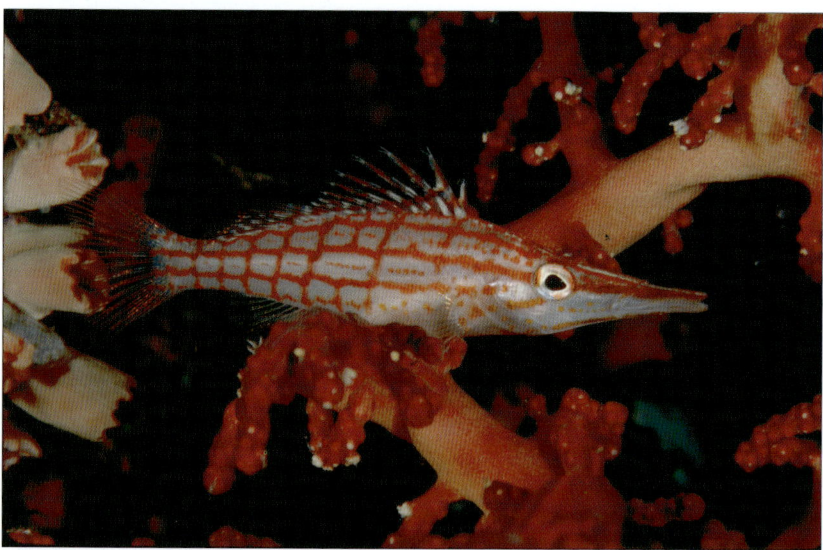

Hawkfish on soft coral. Kodachrome 64 was used to record the detail of reflections from the fish's scales and fins. The film is almost as sharp as Kodachrome 25, and the contrast is excellent. The rule of diagonal composition is definitely broken here. **(Nikon F3; PKR; 105mm Micro Nikkor Lens; Nikonos SB-105 and SB-103 strobes; 1/60 second at *f*16)**

   Essentials of Underwater Photography

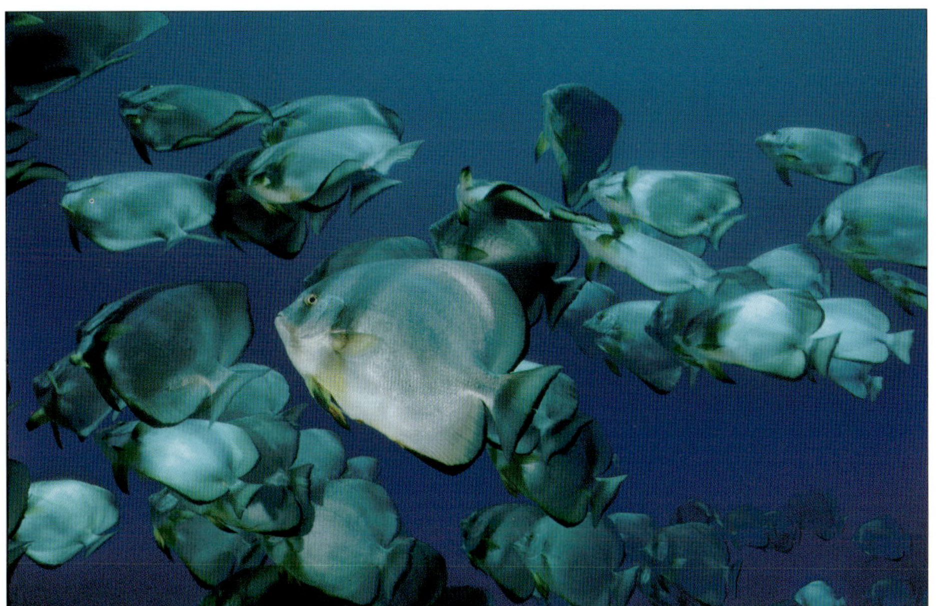

School of bat fish at Ras Mohammed in the Red Sea. The fish were photographed using Kodachrome 200 film, so that the blue water and strobe light were nearly balanced. Although the film shows more grain than the other Kodachromes, the edges are sharp and the detail appears good. The film is warm and fast enough to capture action, like moving fish. **(Nikon F3; PKL; available light with fill-in strobe; 17mm lens; two Sea and Sea YS-200 strobes on 1/2 power; 1/60 second at ƒ11)**

Relatively simple processing with prepackaged chemicals means that E-6 development is available worldwide, even in relatively underdeveloped countries. E-6 processing is simple and often available in the field, including shipboard laboratories. Some underdeveloped countries (for economic reasons) may not adequately control release of chemicals into the ocean. Chemicals used to process E-6 films may be dumped on the very reef the beauty of which is being communicated.

Fuji Velvia (ISO 50) is a high contrast, vividly saturated color slide film that is a favorite for macro and close-up photography. Velvia produces saturated greens and reds, and so it is often useful in landscape photography. Velvia film has some notable idiosyncrasies. It tolerates overexposure much better than underexposure, and its working ISO speed is usually considered 40 or 45, so only trial and error finds the actual exposure. The film has high contrast, which increases if pushed to ISO 80 - 100. Velvia can be pushed roughly 1/3 stop with the exposure meter set at ISO 64. Velvia also may produce ruddy "sunburned" faces in sunlight portraits, although this is not a concern under water.

Some Films Useful for Underwater Photography

Film	ISO	Characteristics	Application	Process
K25 (PKM)	25	Saturated warm colors, extremely fine grain, high sharpness and resolving power	Close-up, macro	K14
K64 (PKR)	64 (80)	Less warm than PKM, dense blacks, extremely fine grain, high sharpness and resolving power	Close-up, macro, open water, general	K14
K200 (PKL)	200	Warm, good edge sharpness, high contrast	Open water, available light or strobe fills, can be push processed to ISO 500-800 range	K14
E100S	100	Saturated neutral colors, fine grain and high sharpness	Macro, general	E-6
E100SW	100	Saturated warm colors, fine grain and high sharpness	Macro, general	E-6
E200SW	200	Saturated warm colors, fine grain and high sharpness, compares favorably to ISO 100 films	Open water, available light or strobe fills, can be push processed to ISO 800	E-6
Velvia	50 (40)	Highly saturated colors, extremely fine grain, high sharpness and resolving power	Macro only, contrast becomes unacceptable if push processed	E-6
Provia	100	Medium speed, good saturation and sharpness	Macro, open water, general photography	E-6
SCALA	200	Medium speed black and white direct positive film, very sharp, wide grey range, visible grain	Open water, available light or strobe fills, can be push processed to ISO 800	Proprietary by Agfa labs

Fuji Provia (ISO 100) is similar to Velvia, although more than one full stop faster. Provia is less saturated and appears slightly more grainy than Velvia. Provia can produce saturated blues in open water, and it frequently appears in publications for that reason. Its medium speed makes it useful for the whole range of macro, close-up, wide-angle strobe, and blue water photography. A consumer version of this film, Sensia, is indistinguishable and costs less.

Ektachrome films were the original E-6 films with EPR-64 as the representative medium speed film. EPR-64 film was fine in grain, low in contrast, and it had a bluish cast (especially on overcast days). A warmer version, EPX-64, was similar but had a warmer color palette. Both films have been replaced by slightly faster (ISO 100), all-purpose Ektachrome films.

Introduced in the early 1990s, Ektachrome Lumiere films had many useful characteristics for underwater photography. Lumiere films incorporated new technology to produce very fine grain. T grain technology permits a sharpness and grain structure comparable to that of K25. The Lumiere films have been replaced by even newer Ektachromes. These films produce pastel colors and have fine grain structure and sharpness. These new Ektachrome films provide a broad range of blue-light capture, due to new spectral capturing dyes.

E100S is an all purpose, medium speed film that produces saturated colors above and below water. It is relatively cool in its color rendition and produces open water blues. E100SW is the warmer version of E100S that also produces saturated reds and red-browns. E100SW produces a clean, open ocean blue and works well with strobe fill to produce warm colors with fill-in flash. E100SW is useful for strobe-filled reef scenics and open water, when the level of ambient light does not require K200.

Storing and Handling Films

Professional films should be stored in original packaging at 55°F (13C) or less in a refrigerator or freezer. Working amounts of film can be kept in unrefrigerated storage for days or even up to a few weeks. Film must be protected from high heat and humidity. According to Kodak, E100SW is especially tolerant of non-refrigerated storage. Films should be processed as soon as possible after exposure to prevent deterioration of the latent image.

Cold film should be kept in the original package (to prevent condensation) until it reaches room temperature. A 35mm film canister requires 1 1/2 to 2 hours to fully acclimate to room temperature.

All films should be protected from x-rays, even several low level doses can degrade the film and alter the latent image. Checked and carry on baggage is all subjected to x-rays. Some new x-ray machines, based on CAT scanning technology, may be especially damaging. High speed films are especially vulnerable to x-ray damage and should be checked in lead bags. Visual inspection can avoid these problems, as can carrying film in heavy-duty lead bags.

Professional films have tighter exposure tolerances. The actual ISO speed is usually very close (within $1/6\,f$ stop) to the nominal speed. Amateur films may differ by as much as $1/3\,f$ stop in either direction ($2/3\,f$ stop total). Professional films require refrigeration or freezing to maintain optimal color balance. These films have short shelf lives, since they are released at optimum color balance. Although accurate color rendition may be less important under water, consistency is important because non-uniform color rendition is distracting. The variety of films available for professional use far exceeds that available for amateur use.

This chapter has emphasized professional films. These are the most cost effective way to achieve consistent exposure and color rendition. Consistent results may not be critical to some photographers, but most working photographers chose professional versions of Kodachrome, Ektachrome, and Fuji films for these reasons.

"The camera trigger was connected by an electric cable to the powder. Sometimes Dr. Longley had to wait two hours before fish would swim into his camera field, while the man above held up the powder, never knowing when Longley would shoot. The boatmen also had to keep rowing after Longley's peregrinations on the bottom. When the charge went off it temporarily blinded them, showering sparks and a cloud of evil smoke. The system was 'more that human nerves could stand,' said Longley."

James Dugan, 1956, <u>Man Under the Sea</u>

Introduction

Strobes are electronic devices that store electrical energy and discharge it extremely rapidly in the form of light. They transfer energy from alkaline cells or rechargeable nickel cadmium batteries to a capacitor, where the energy accumulates. The capacitor releases stored energy as light from the flash tube, a glass cylinder filled with ionizable gas. The discharge of light peaks rapidly and lasts for only a few thousandths of a second.

The important parts of a strobe have not changed since development before WWII by Harold Edgerton, an electrical engineer. A relatively low voltage battery can serve as the power source. Most modern strobes use rechargeable nickel-cadmium batteries, although many available flashes can also use disposable batteries. One or more capacitors gather electrical energy

A circuit diagram of a simple electronic strobe, designed by Harold Edgerton.

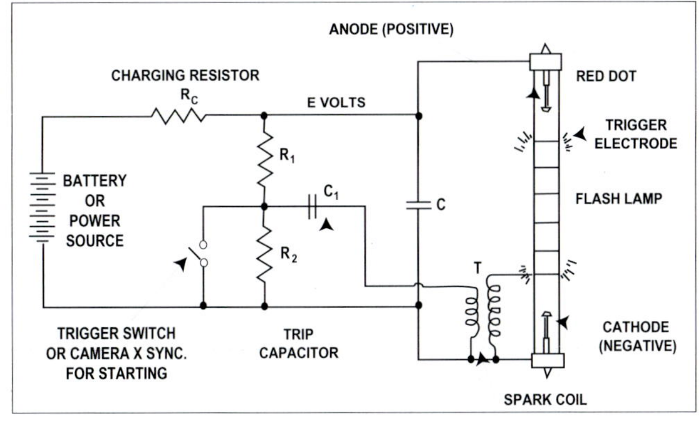

over time from the battery. Capacitors rapidly discharge large amounts of energy, which can be dangerous. (Similar devices are used in cardiac defibrillators and an inadvertent discharge can actually cause fibrillation.) Resistors, diodes, rectifiers, and transformers in various combinations make up the rest of the circuit. A switch controls the on-off function, and a neon tube shows when the capacitor is charged.

After WWII, Edgerton made photographs and worked with Jacques-Yves Cousteau. Many of these early strobe photographs (taken both with scuba and deep ocean instrument sleds) were published in the *National Geographic*. Later, Edgerton formed a company (EG&G) that temporarily marketed compact, waterproof strobes for use with underwater cameras like the Rolleimarin and Nikonos (Calypso). An example, the EG&G model 211, appeared in <u>Camera Below</u> in 1968, along with a complete circuit diagram for do-it-yourself strobe builders. The only important innovation since that time has been the addition of TTL or matrix automatic exposure circuitry, which sometimes permits more accurate flash exposures.

Strobe Power

Strobe power is normally described in "watt-seconds," but this number does not provide enough information to predict the correct exposure. Strobes can be given a guide number, which reflects the correct exposure for a given ISO at a certain distance. Within limits, guide numbers can be used to calculate approximate exposures. In practice, watt-second ratings are only "nominal." Many other factors really determine both the correct exposure and useful coupling range.

The actual light output of a strobe depends on its watt-second power rating, material, and shape of the reflector, area of coverage, and capacitor charge. Predicting exposure based on GN, strobe tables supplied by the manufacturer or measuring output using a flash meter is, at best, only a starting point. Only trial and error reveals the best exposure for a given situation.

Strobe intensity decreases with distance because the area of coverage increases. The decrease is estimated in air by the inverse square law, which describes the light falloff with distance from a point source. The inverse square law fails to predict correct exposures in water because of light diffusion by suspended particles, strobe placement angles, and because the light source is not a single point.

Power output can vary with the charge of the capacitor (i.e., power is less if the capacitor is not fully formed). Battery discharge can affect the final power output by decreasing the rate of capacitor charging.

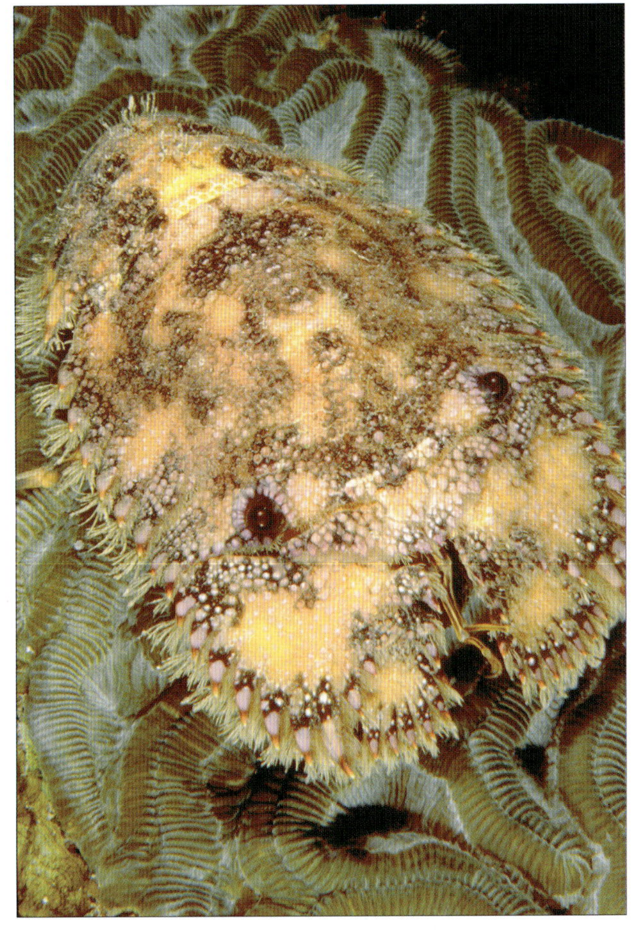

Recycle time (usually several seconds) varies among strobes but it is, in general, less than 30 seconds. The ready light of many strobes glows *before* fully charging the capacitor, so triggering the flash early will result in less power. This can sometimes be exploited to reduce strobe output in fill-in flash situations, all be it unpredictably.

More important, the light beam of a strobe varies in shape, depending on geometry of the reflector. Strobes that have narrow beams need less power output to illuminate a smaller surface area. Narrow beam strobes are useful for macrophotography where they can be used in pairs to provide strong but balanced lighting. Wide beam strobes (examples include the Sea and Sea YS-300 and the Nikonos SB104) distribute light over a much larger surface area and so require more power output. The reflector surface also affects the light output of the strobe. Reflectors vary in color from white to highly reflective silvered plastic.

The color of light produced varies from strobe to strobe. Some produce warmer light (e.g., Nikonos SB-104) while others provide cooler (e.g., SR2000) light. The color temperature of light indicates how light produced by a strobe corresponds to color produced by a heated iron ball. At extremely high temperatures, the ball glows white, a condition described as "cold" light. At lower temperatures, it glows orange or red, a condition described as "warm." Referring to the light output of a strobe as red or blue is more descriptive.

Color temperature of strobes can change as the power output varies. Very short exposures, e.g., TTL strobe used at short distances, produces a cold light (less red, more blue). Diffusers (see below) can change the color of light produced by strobes. White plastic typically warms (more red) the light produced, but the actual color shift depends on the material used.

Manual Strobe Exposures

Strobes can be used in a "manual" mode, i.e., the exposure set by hand, or in an "automatic" mode (TTL) in which the camera's internal meter circuit signals the strobe to limit output. Because basic photographic techniques are so important to successful underwater photography, this book stresses manual exposure techniques.

In manual strobe photography, the aperture (not shutter speed) determines the exposure. Underwater photographers cannot rely on guide numbers or strobe tables provided by manufacturers, but rather should establish correct exposures for each strobe-distance combination by testing in water. This means setting up the camera (say with a 105-mm lens) and dual strobes and taking a series of exposures at 1/2 stop increments until the "correct" (subjectively most desirable) exposure is found. The goal can be accomplished in a swimming pool (preferably at night to decrease background light) using a test target. Exposures should be at 1/2-stop intervals, e.g., starting at $f32$, $f22\ 1/2$, $f22$, $f16\ 1/2$, $f16$, $f11\ 1/2$ ... and so on, so that when they develop the film the correct exposure can be found. Test strips should be left unmounted. An example of a strobe table follows:

Film: E100sw   **Lens: 105mm**   **Strobe(s): 2SB-105's**

.5 ft	notes	1 ft	notes	1.5 ft	notes	2 ft	notes
32	under	32	under	22	under	22	under
22.5	OK	22.5	under	16.5	under	16.5	under
22	OK+	22	under	16	OK	16	under
16.5	over	16.5	OK	11.5	OK+	11.5	under
16	over	16	OK+	11	over	11	OK

Even after careful testing, the actual exposure that appears most correct can vary in the sea because of reflectiveness of the subject. Exposures of critical subjects should always be bracketed, even after the test exposures.

Correct exposure is an arbitrary choice, but some conventions apply. First, slide films favor underexposure, so always expose for the highlights. In contrast print films, which are not often used under water, favor overexposure. So, always expose for the shadows.

Bracketing Strobe Exposures

Although most manual strobes have adjustable power, output bracketing is necessary to achieve correct exposures when shooting with strobe-balanced light. These techniques can be used in macrophotography (full light provided by the strobe) or in wide-angle photography (in which the strobe fills in the shadows.) The light output of a manual strobe can be varied by changing the power setting (full, 1/2, 1/4, etc.), using a diffuser, or changing the distance from strobe to subject.

TTL (Automatic) Strobe Exposure

Through-the-lens (TTL) automatic exposure strobes usually receive a signal from the camera body meter and computer indicating when to stop burning. Peak power of the flash tube output remains nearly constant, so duration of the flash is used to control how much light the strobe produces. The TTL system works well and produces accurate exposures based on programmed film speed (ISO setting), aperture (f stop), and average reflectance. Useful TTL apertures can vary widely because strobe power is adjustable over a wide range. This is not the case with manual strobes, which typically have 1/2, 1/4, and 1/8 power settings.

Shutter speed is not important unless it is shorter than the fastest synchronization speed (e.g., 1/60 second) for the strobe and camera body. Enough time must exist for the film surface to be fully exposed between leaves of the shutter moving across the film surface in parallel. The movement may be horizontal or vertical, depending on the camera model. The standard synchronization speed was 1/60 second, but in modern cameras synchronization can be as fast as 1/250 second.

In TTL systems, the film speed dial can be used to adjust the TTL system independent of aperture and shutter speed. To decrease light output, the film speed is increased. Increasing the film speed setting on the body by one stop (for example from 100 to 200) decreases the light output of a TTL strobe by 50%. Smaller decreases allow more accurate adjustment of the amount of light reaching the film plane. If the ISO control of the camera can be reached under water (as with the Nikonos V), this adjustment can be a useful way to bracket TTL exposures.

TTL strobe-camera-film units are limited to a certain useful range of distances (the "coupling range") based on power output of the strobe and film speed. The coupling range is usually indicated on printed tables supplied by strobe manufacturers. This table also gives minimum and maximum apertures for any given strobe to subject distance.

TTL strobes are usually equipped with full power warning indicators. This is a warning light that fires when the strobe has used its full capacitor charge. It may mean underexposure, but an acceptable exposure could also have occurred. Slide film tends to favor underexposure, so the "full dump" could still produce an acceptably exposed image. The remedy is to open the aperture (which decreases depth of field) or move the strobe closer to the subject.

Although they function automatically, unpredictable situations can and do occur, so TTL strobes also require bracketing. The film speed indicator (ISO setting dial) can be used to bracket TTL exposures as described above. TTL strobes are sometimes used at -1/3 to -2/3 exposure compensation to prevent burnout of highlights on slide films.

Matrix Exposure Systems

Matrix flash is a special kind of TTL flash that can provide fill-in lighting by measuring the ambient light in the background. A camera and strobe must be designed to work together in the matrix metering mode. Some strobes designed for use above water (e.g., Nikon SB-26) are capable of exposure compensation in the matrix mode.

Matrix metering systems tend to increase the exposure of a central subject (that is usually darker) relative to the background (usually lighter). The camera must be set to matrix metering. Using aperture priority, the shutter speed is adjusted to between 1/60 and 1/250 second. If the flash symbol blinks after release, then the frame may be underexposed and a wider aperture should be chosen. The coupling range for each aperture must be considered, giving several possible apertures for any distance chosen. Bracketing and exposure compensation to keep the foreground subject properly exposed are still necessary.

Dual Strobes

Symmetrical lighting produced by dual strobes usually produces more pleasing results than just a single strobe. A single strobe produces harsh shadows, while balanced lighting produces flatter, more evenly illuminated lighting.

Pleasing images result from one dominant strobe that is either more powerful or positioned closer. This creates slightly asymmetrical lighting (i.e., it allows the light to have a direction) and increases contrast.

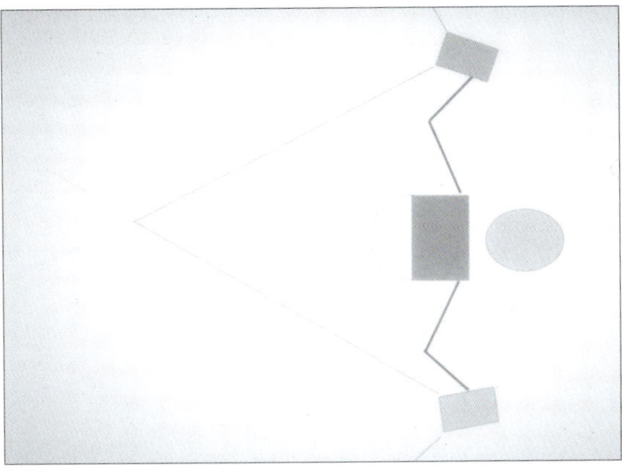

Diagram of proper strobe position for wide-angle and fill-in strobe lighting. The view is from above. Long strobe arms are needed. The strobes should be BEHIND the housing, and they can even be "toed out" slightly. This position minimizes backscatter and prevents a wide-angle lens from "seeing" the strobes.

Dual strobe lighting can be done with two strobes of equal intensity or with two strobes of different powers. The use of equally powered strobes produces shadowless, symmetrical lighting. Strobes of different power allow more dramatic lighting, but detail is still lost in shadows. Dual strobes can be triggered several ways. Strobes can be connected via a T connector to the strobe fitting of a Nikonos or the bulkhead connector of a housing. This arrangement allows use of equal or unequal strobes in manual or TTL modes. Otherwise, strobes may be connected to two independent bulkhead fittings (by separate cords), providing a backup if one cord should fail. One strobe may also be used as the primary strobe that is connected by wire to the camera, while another operates in the slave mode. The slave does not require a wire connection to the camera. Strobes may contain built-in slave circuitry, or can be triggered by connection to remote slave sensors. Some slave sensors (e.g., Ikelite) also allow the strobes to operate in the TTL mode.

The power of strobes is not additive, because many factors, including position, influence the aperture for correct exposure. Ideally, if two strobes were points of light coming from the same spot, one could calculate a final guide number as the geometric means of the guide numbers, e.g., GNtotal = $\sqrt{([GN_1]^2 + [GN_2]^2)}$, and so on. Strobes are not point sources, nor are they ever in the same position, so careful, in-water testing is always necessary to find the correct exposure.

Strobes in Wide-angle Photography

Wide beam, large strobes (like the Ikelite SS200, Sea and See YS-300, and Nikonos SB-104) are required for wide-angle photography (35mm and shorter focal length lenses). Wide-angle strobe photography usually involves fill-in lighting with the overall exposure controlled by the amount of ambient light. Correct exposure based on balanced strobe power and ambient light is difficult and depends on relative strobe power and other variables. Strobe positioning is critical when working with extreme wide-angle lenses in dome ports or extreme wide-angle lenses on the Nikonos (15 mm or 12 mm).

Long, freely movable strobe arms (e.g., Ikelite, Ultralight, TLC, or Ocean Bright) make positioning the strobe easier and more consistent. Usually, strobes should be at least 4 - 6 feet apart for wide-angle photography. Strobes must be positioned behind the housing with the beams angled slightly outward, as shown on page 45. In this way, the less intense edges of the beams overlap in the center of the frame, creating a more evenly lighted scene. The outward angle of the beams prevents lighting the water directly in front of the lens, so particles and the debris are not visible.

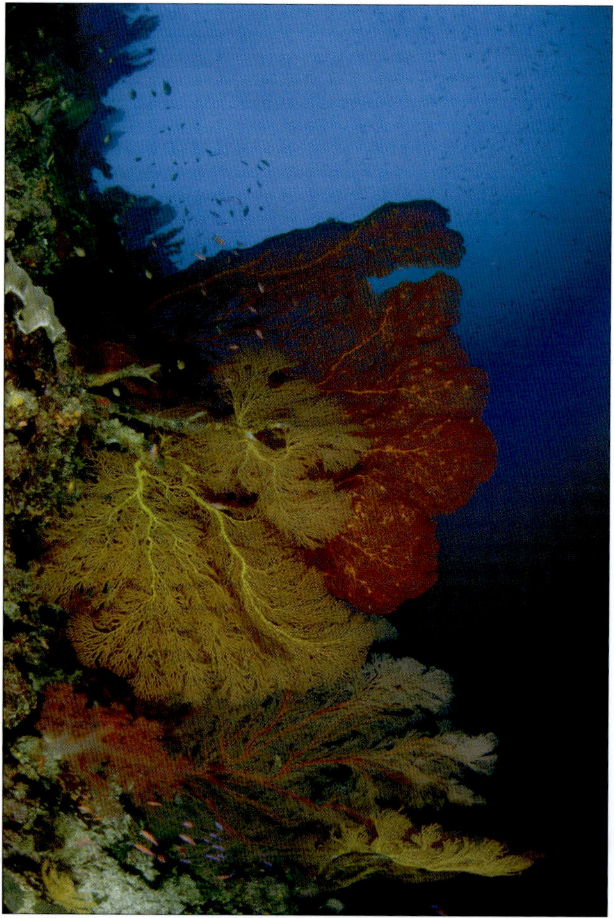

Reef "scenic" shot with combined available light and fill-in strobes. The fan coral is entirely illuminated by the strobes, which balance the available sunlight. One f stop diffusers were placed over the strobes, and the right strobe was aimed away. The photograph was made late in the day, and the sun was not strong. The warm orange-browns of the coral are conveyed well by the Ektachrome Lumiere film. **(Nikon F3; LPZ; 16mm lens; two Sea and Sea YS-200 strobes; 1/60 second at f4)**

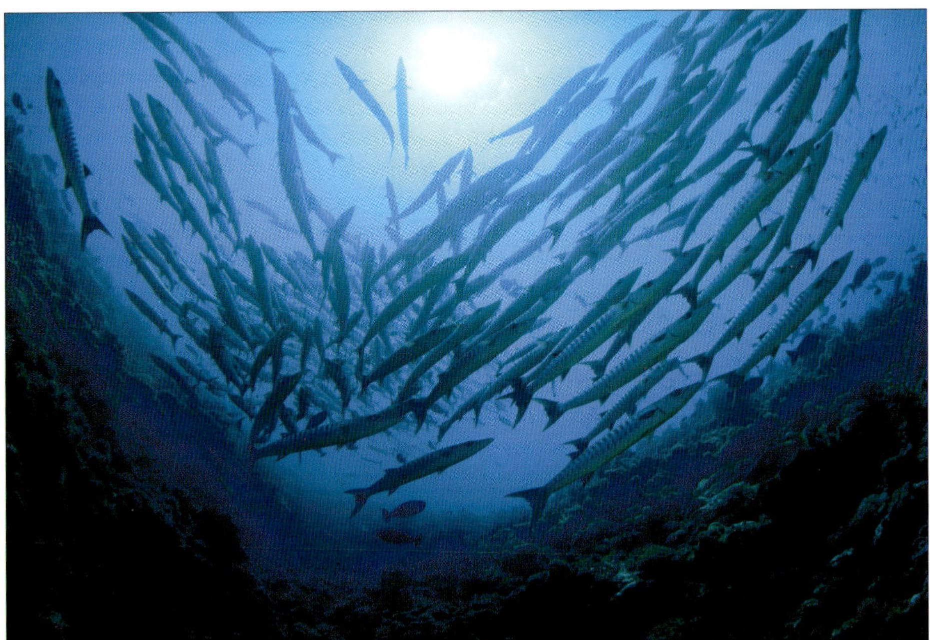

Schooling barracuda in available light with fill-in strobe. The angle of view is upwards, and the sunlight would produce a silhouette without the strobes. The artificial light very gently lit the undersides of the barracuda. The school produces a gently curving diagonal area across the frame. **(Nikon F3; LPZ 100; available light with fill-in strobe; 16mm lens; two Sea and Sea YS-200 strobes on 1/2 power; 1/60 second at *f*8)**

Balanced Lighting

Strobes used for balanced lighting should be matched wide beam units. Using two strobes of different power or decreasing one strobe's power creates less even lighting. Balanced lighting implies that ambient light is enough for background exposure. Balanced lighting provides strobe lighting of the point of interest, roughly equal to the ambient light. The amount of available light in midwater usually controls the correct background exposure. The challenge is to adjust the power of the strobe or move the strobe to produce a strobe exposure equal to the background light.

The light meter (it is best to use a separate spot meter) or the camera body's meter (set on spot metering) is aimed at a point in the midwater column. Neither the sun (underexposure), nor the bottom (overexposure) should be metered. The midwater column can be underexposed to increase color saturation (especially with Ektachrome films).

The aperture is based on the meter reading and a strobe synch speed, usually 1/60 - 1/250 second (although longer exposures can

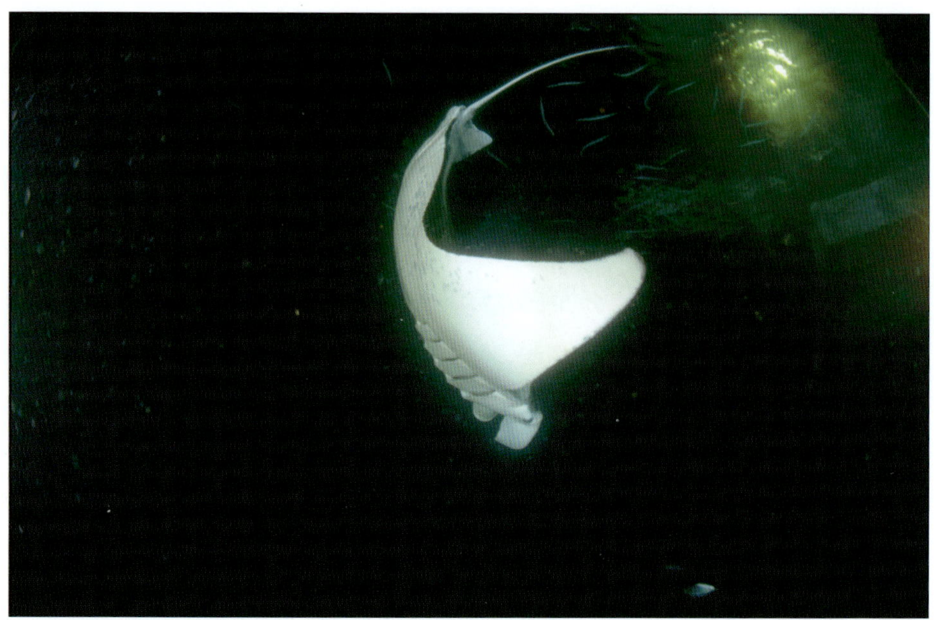

A manta photographed at night with full strobe lighting. The exposure was for the underside of the manta, so that the water appears black (although it was lighted by floodlights). The sensation of motion is provided by the curve of the manta's body. Detail in the nearest wing is lost because of overexposure. **(Nikon F3; LPZ 100; 16mm lens; two Sea and Sea YS-200 strobes on 1/2 power; 1/60 second at $f8$)**

possibly be used) is chosen. The settings depend on film speed, so becoming familiar with a single film is useful. The strobe-to-subject distance can be estimated. Since this is almost always < 3 feet, it is easy to memorize f stops for 1, 2, and 3 feet. The strobe is positioned facing the object of interest.

For example, if the background exposure is $f11$ at 1/60 second (this is the meter reading) and the strobe power requires $f8$ at 1/60 second, the strobe must be moved closer. If the background is $f8$ at 1/60 second but the strobe power requires $f11$ at 1/60 second, the strobe power must be decreased by adding a 1 f stop diffuser (probably the best option) or moving the strobe back (double the distance). The photographer then composes the picture, maintains a comfortable position, and takes the photograph.

If the background is poorly lit and the required aperture is large, e.g., $f2.8$, the photograph can still sometimes be made by slowing the shutter speed to 1/30 or even 1/15 second. Learning how to control these camera functions allows powerful control of both flash and ambient light exposures.

 Essentials of Underwater Photography

Balanced Lighting with TTL

TTL techniques are similar but are certainly not automatic. First, a light meter is used to meter the midwater column. The aperture is then set based on the meter reading (usually at a shutter speed of <1/250 second). The coupling range is important because the strobe must be placed within a usable coupling range. If strobe power is too little at the distance chosen (based on coupling range), the strobe should be moved closer to the subject.

Using this technique does not allow bracketing by changing ISO setting of the camera. Changing the ISO affects both strobe output and exposure of the film. TTL techniques work best when ambient light is relatively low. If the camera is set to manual, bracketing can be done by adjusting the ISO so that shutter speed and aperture can be controlled separately from the strobe.

Flooded Strobes

Disassembling strobes can be dangerous, since electrical shocks can occur, especially if sea water has entered the strobe. Although flooded

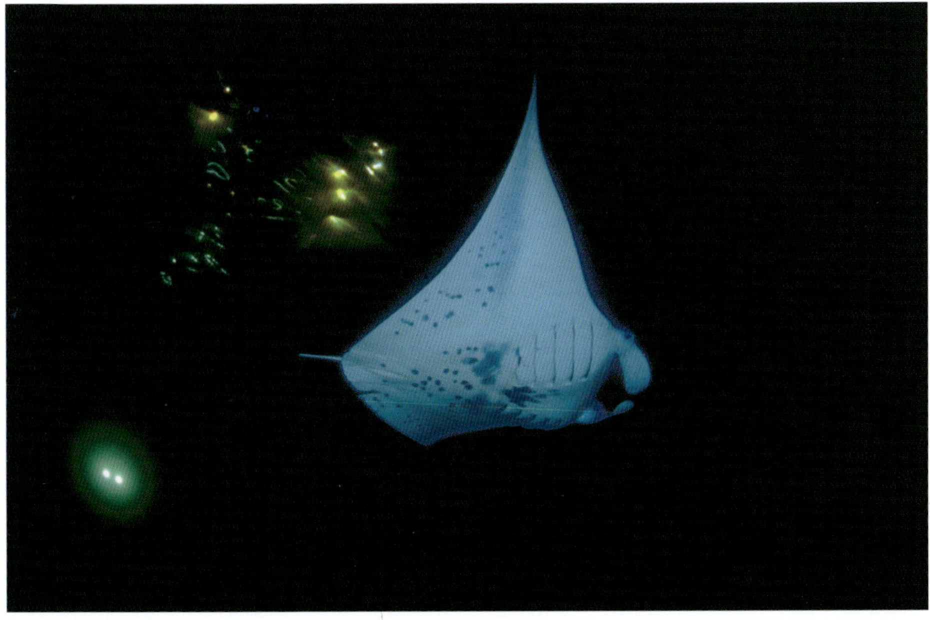

A manta photographed at night with full strobe lighting. Slight underexposure brings out detail in the white underside of the manta. The manta here is further from the strobes. **(Nikon F3; LPZ 100; available light with fill-in strobe; 16mm lens; two Sea and Sea YS-200 strobes on 1/2 power; 1/60 second at ƒ11)**

strobes can possibly be salvaged, if they do not function normally after a freshwater rinse and drying at engine room temperature, they probably are not worth repairing. Imagine expecting your television set or PC to operate normally after submersion in sea water. Production of hydrogen gas during charging of the batteries is another possible hazard of strobes. Strobes can also produce explosive gases if the battery floods and electrolysis occurs because of short circuiting.

"A motorcycle may be divided for purposes of classical rational analysis by means of its component assemblies and by means of its functions."

Robert M. Pirsig, 1974,
Zen and the Art of Motorcycle Maintenance

Macrophotography Defined

In this chapter, close-up photography is any photography in which strobe light provides essentially all illumination at a short (one- to two-foot) working distance from the camera. Macrophotography is defined by the magnification ratio, and strobes still provide all light. Magnification ratios of 1:3 and greater (1:2 and 1:1) define the macrorange and usually require very short working distances.

Macrophotography requires being physically close to the subject. Advantages include minimizing the amount of water and suspended material between the lens and the subject and filling the frame. Disadvantages include the possibility of touching or disturbing the subject and possible damage to the reef. It is also difficult to creatively deal with negative space when there is so little of it.

Equipment for Macrophotography

Close-up or macrophotographs can be made using a variety of equipment, including macrolenses, extension tubes, and add-on close-up lenses. Each of these approaches will be discussed. Most emphasis is placed on housed 35mm cameras used in the manual mode, since this approach demonstrates the best basic photographic principles used in any photography.

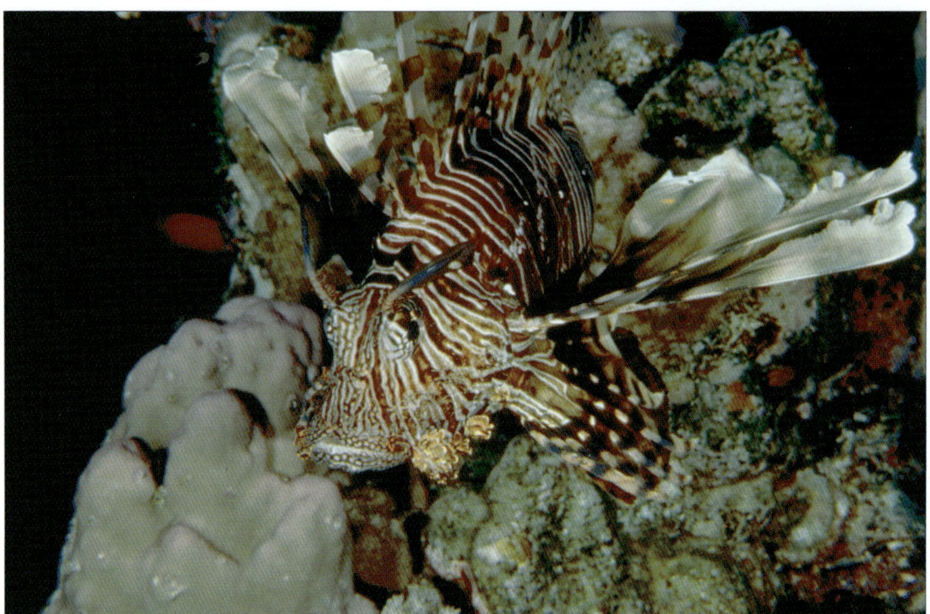

Lionfish photographed as a close-up portrait. The fish swam toward the camera and then gestured by twisting its head. The camera was prefocused and ready to fire. Frequently, behaviors like this that appear unique are actually repetitive. Knowing this allows planning the shot and repeating it until it is right. **(Nikon F3; LPZ; 105mm lens; Nikonos SB-105 and SB-103 strobes; 1/60 second at ƒ8)**

Nikonos Extension Tubes and Close-up Lenses

Extension tubes function specifically with the Nikonos camera. These are water-tight tubes that are placed between the primary (35mm) lens and the camera body. These are usually machined from aluminum, but may also be fabricated from plastic. Tubes are usually designed so that magnification ratios of 1: 3, 1: 2, and 1: 1 can be accomplished using different lengths. The longest tubes produce the highest magnification. Longer tubes move the aperture farther from the film plane and decrease the effective aperture. A lens at $f22$ may act like a lens set at $f32$, or even $f64$, depending on the length of the tube. The result is a need for more light with long extension tubes (the "bellows effect"). The decrease in the depth of field (zone of acceptable focus) that occurs with long extension tubes is another significant consideration. Tubes long enough to give 1: 1 magnification may yield a zone of acceptable focus of only a few millimeters. Essentially, only a plane can be photographed, e.g., a flat coral surface.

The lack of through-the-lens focusing creates another problem in the Nikonos system that is magnified by the use of extension tubes. Composition is difficult and requires use of a mechanical framer,

Essentials of Underwater Photography

usually constructed of wire. Framers may shift position (or may not be positioned properly in the first place). True placement can be determined only by trial and error, e.g., by photographing a known pattern. The mechanical nature of framers also makes them subject to accident. They may become bent or misshapen by rough handling.

Close-up Lenses

Close-up lenses are described in "diopters." The diopter number (e.g., +1, etc.) refers to 1000 divided by the focal length of the close-up lens. For example, a +2 diopter lens will have a focal length 500mm (it will focus at 500mm or 19.7 inches). Higher diopter numbers focus closer.

Close-up lenses can be used on lenses in housed cameras and on Nikonos cameras. Close-up lenses used in housed cameras are added to the primary lens and are available in a range of magnifications. These lenses are rarely used under water. Primary lenses for which the close-up lenses are intended frequently do not focus near enough to permit their use at a close distance.

Close-up lenses increase maximum magnification by decreasing the farthest distance at which an object is in focus. So, close-up lenses

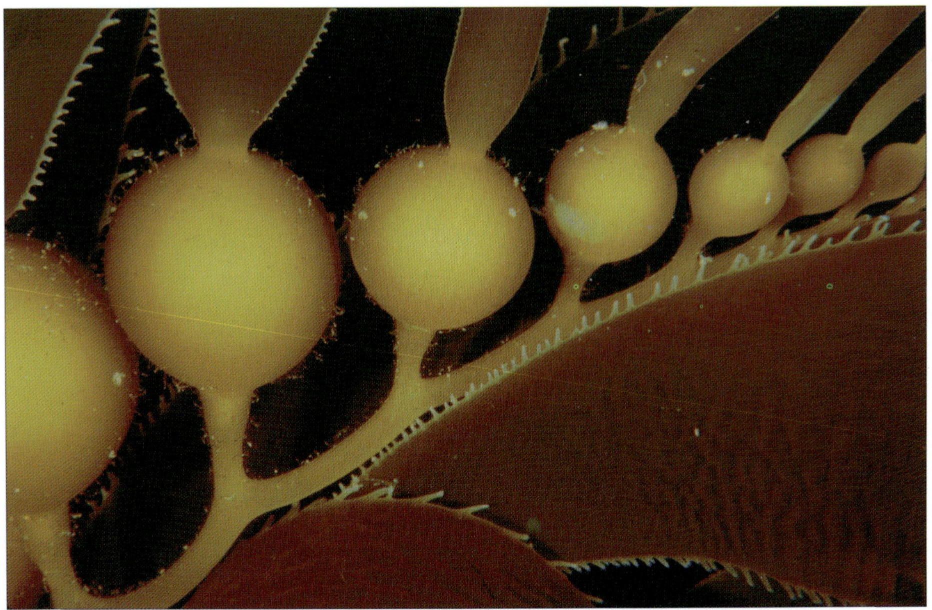

Detail of kelp frond shot in macro. The photograph combines elements of composition including the diagonally placed curved line and decreasing size of the cysts, which creates visual interest. **(Nikon F3; EPP; 105mm lens; Nikonos SB-105 and SB-103 strobes; 1/60 second at ƒ8)**

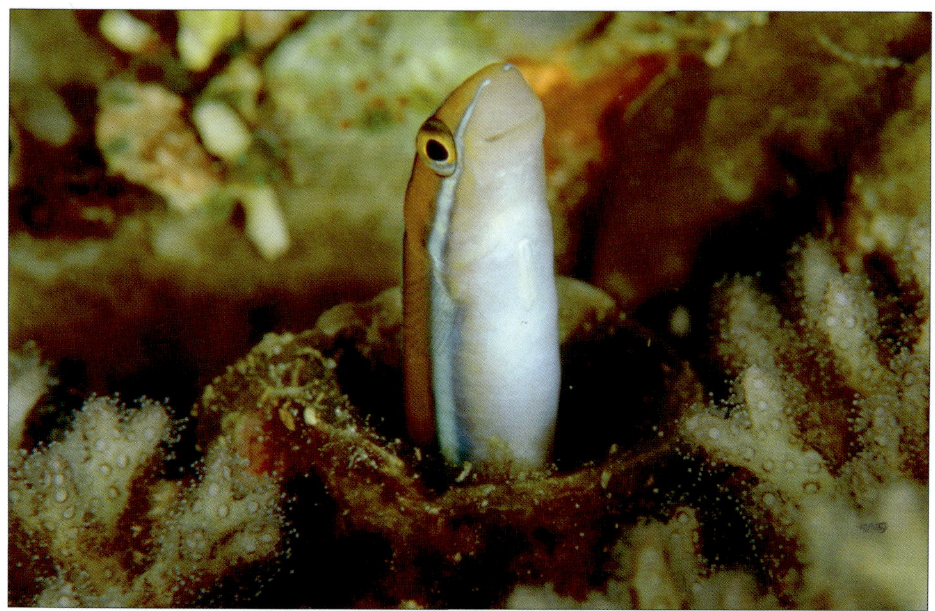

Goby emerging from a coral head. The photograph is a typical macro shot, made interesting by the "smile" on the fish's "face." **(Nikon F3; LPZ; SB-105 and SB-103 strobes on full manual; 105mm lens with 1.4x TC; 1/60 second at ƒ16)**

lend the ability to photograph a somewhat closer object at the expense of being unable to focus on infinity. Close-up lenses do not change the amount of light entering the film plane appreciably. They do permit a greater magnification at closer working distances.

Macro Lenses

Macrophotography (more so than close-up) requires critically accurate focus. This is evident with long lenses (105mm and 200mm), since the zone of acceptable focus may be only a few millimeters. Macrophotography is best done with a single lens reflex camera.

Close-up photography can be done with any lens that focuses to about two feet or less, including extreme wide-angle lenses. Typical close-up lenses like the 60mm Micro Nikkor lens have a narrow angle of view. Extreme wide-angle lenses generally result in close focus on a specific subject, which may be positioned at the center or edge of the composition, with negative space filled with blue water as background.

Macrolenses usually focus in the range of 1:3 to 1: 1 or even 2: 1. In this ratio, the first number refers to the image size and the second number refers to the size of the object. At a ratio of 1: 3, a 3 cm object would be 1 cm in length on the film plane.

Essentials of Underwater Photography

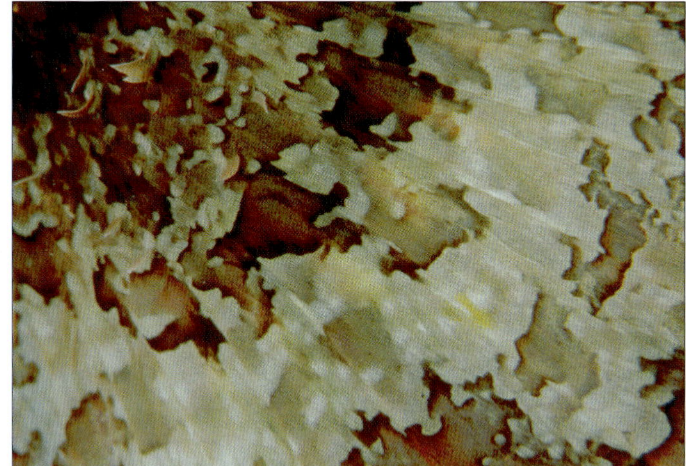

Detail of a scorpionfish pectoral fin. This is a version of a shot I have taken many times. This one has texture and strong diagonals that help the composition. The detail is extreme. **(Nikon F3; PKR at 80; SB-105 and SB-103 strobes on full manual; 105mm lens with 2x TC; 1/60 second at _f_16)**

Working distance is an important consideration in the choice of macrolenses. Longer focal length lenses typically have longer working distances and make photography of nervous animals and even lighting of subjects easier.

Since macrophotography requires full strobe illumination, the focal length of the lens influences how the subject will be lighted. Short macrolenses like the 60mm Micro Nikkor can require extreme strobe angles, e.g. nearly vertical lighting ("high key"), because the lens port is so near the subject. In contrast the 105mm and 200mm lenses allow more natural lighting with dual strobes at the edges of the frame.

Teleconverters

Teleconverters are a cost effective way of increasing the focal length of a macrolens. Nikon teleconverters are available for the 60mm and 105mm lenses. The optics of the Nikon teleconverters are excellent and provide sharp edge to edge images. Both the 1.4x and the 2x teleconverters can operate in housings, and they provide full aperture and focus control. Some after-market teleconverters do not provide such excellent sharpness and can result in significant image quality degradation.

Viewfinders

Few modern cameras are equipped with an Action Finder. These are really irreplaceable for underwater photography. The Nikon F3, F4, and F5 cameras have large optional viewfinders that can replace the standard prism.

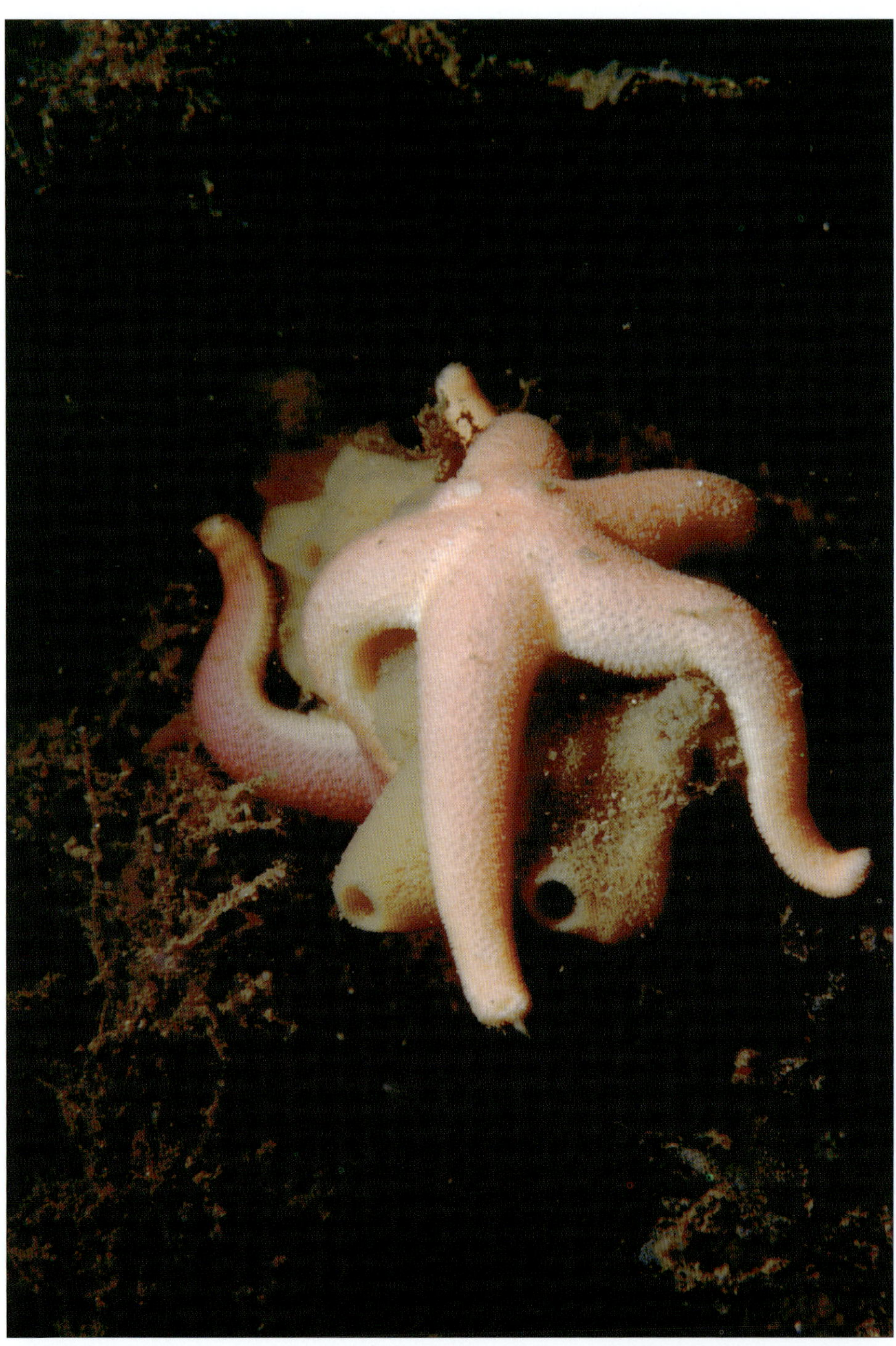

High key lighting demonstrated by an old photograph made with a single strobe. Note the harsh "overhead" lighting and strong shadows under the blood sea stars on the sponge. **(Nikon F; Kodachrome 64; 55mm lens; Honeywell Strobonar 770 strobe on full manual; 1/60 second at ƒ16)**

Essentials of Underwater Photography

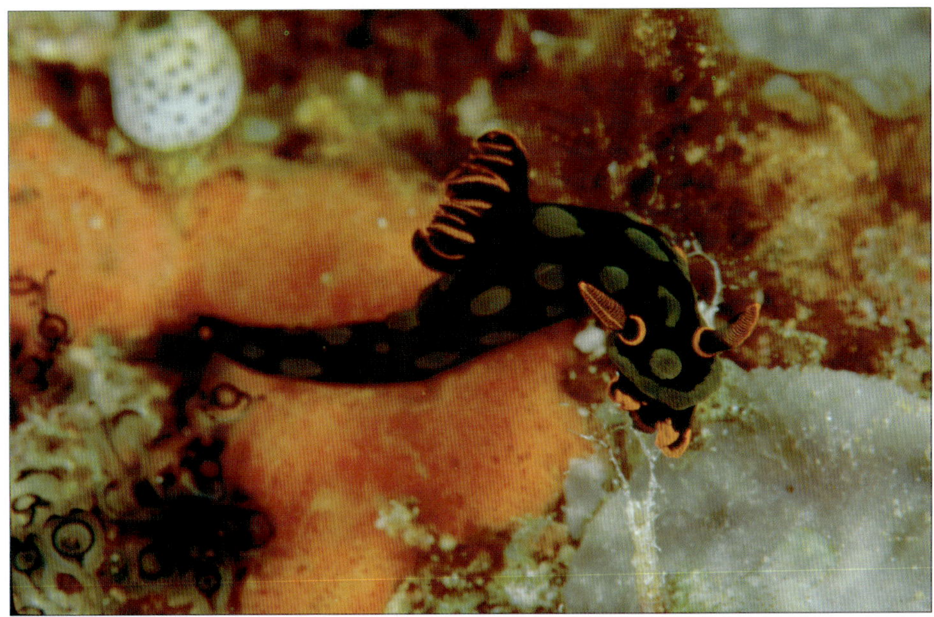

Nembrotha nudibranch. The point of interest is to the right of the frame, and only the rhinopores are in sharp focus. The lighting is even and hence somewhat flat. **(Nikon F3; LPZ; SB-105 and SB-103 strobes on full manual; 105mm lens with 1.4x TC; 1/60 second at ƒ16)**

These are valuable for precise focus and composition. Autofocus cameras are usually not equipped with Action Finders. Autofocus cameras typically require a reducing lens, e.g., the SuperEye, to see the full view finder through the housing. The resulting image is tiny and makes manual focus difficult.

The image in the Action Finder is usually sufficiently bright to permit critical focusing. If it is not, one can

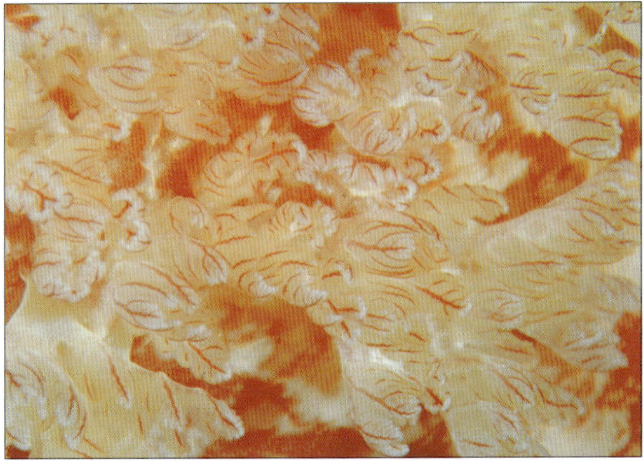

Spanish dancer gill detail. The pattern is abstract (i.e., it's not easily identified as part of a whole) and the detail and texture are strong elements. Colors appear richly saturated and the gill edges are sharp. The detail is highlighted by the white edges of the gill "feathers." **(Nikon F3; LPZ 100; 105mm Micro Nikkor lens with 2x TC; two Nikonos SB-105 strobes; 1/60 second at ƒ 11)**

mount an accessory light on the camera housing or on a strobe arm. The accessory light should have a wide, strong, bright beam that does not

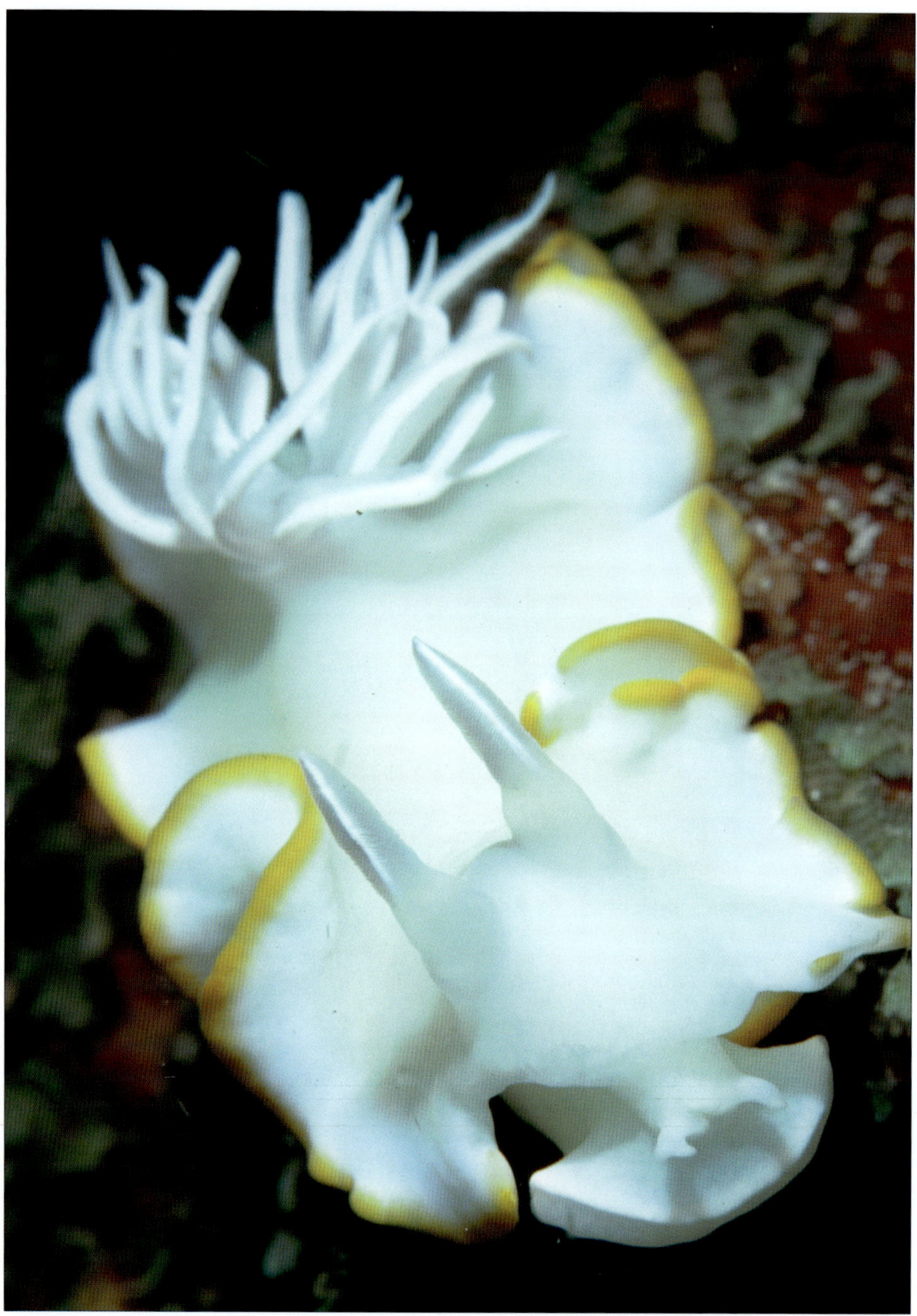

This dorid nudibranch was photographed in the Solomon Islands. I used dual Nikonos strobes and a Nikon 105mm Micro Nikkor lens with 1.4x teleconverter. The film was professional Kodachrome 64. The original image appears sharp and essentially grain free. Important aspects of the composition are the low angle (looking up at the rhinopores) and the diagonal placement of the subject. **(Nikon F3; PKR at 80; SB-105 and SB-103 strobes on full manual; 105mm lens with 1.4x TC; 1/60 second at ƒ16)**

Essentials of Underwater Photography

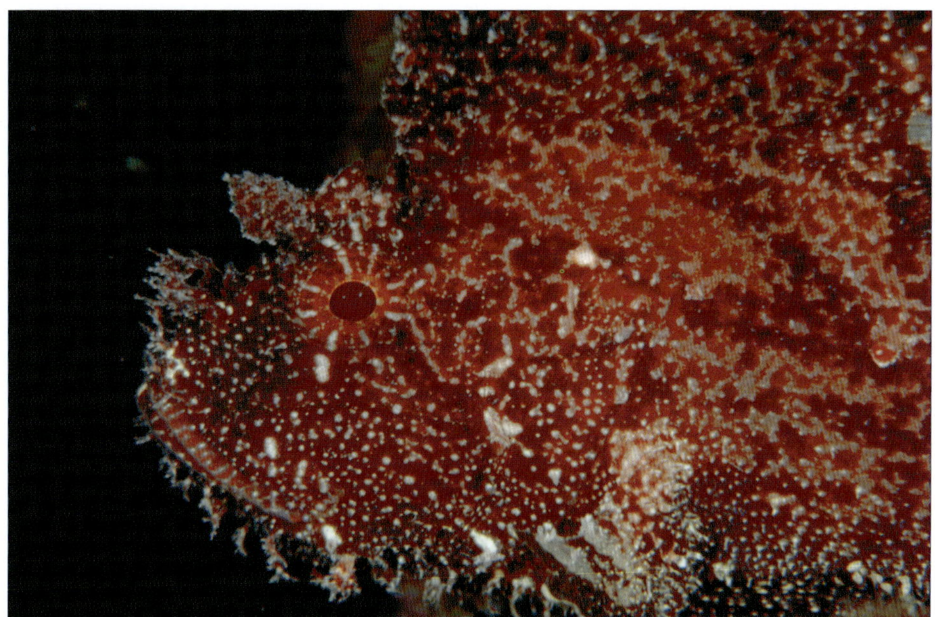

Leaf scorpionfish at night. This is one of several exposures that bracketed composition and strobe exposures. The dark surface of the fish did not reflect much light so the color is well-saturated. **(Nikon F3; LPZ 100; 105mm Micro Nikkor lens with 2x TC; two Nikonos SB-105 strobes; 1/60 second at f11)**

have a hot spot. It should not be so bright that it frightens light sensitive animals. One approach to this problem is to use a diffuser over the accessory light. The camera viewfinder screen can also be replaced with an after-market product (Beattie Screen) that is more efficient and brighter.

Strobe Lighting

Most macrophotography depends on strobe illumination. Two **balanced** strobes (small strobes are OK) are required for even illumination. TTL strobe exposure is excellent for most macrophotography. Manual (non-automatic) strobe exposure usually works well and has the added advantage of bracketing. The basic exposure can be determined by trial and error during construction of a strobe table as described in Chapter 6.

Using manual exposure, distance is estimated and an exposure chosen. The first exposure should be at the "correct exposure." The next exposure should be 1/2 f stop (generally slide film should be underexposed) and finally +1/2 f stop. Wider bracketing can be done if desired, but this usually suffices if an exposure table has been made prior to diving.

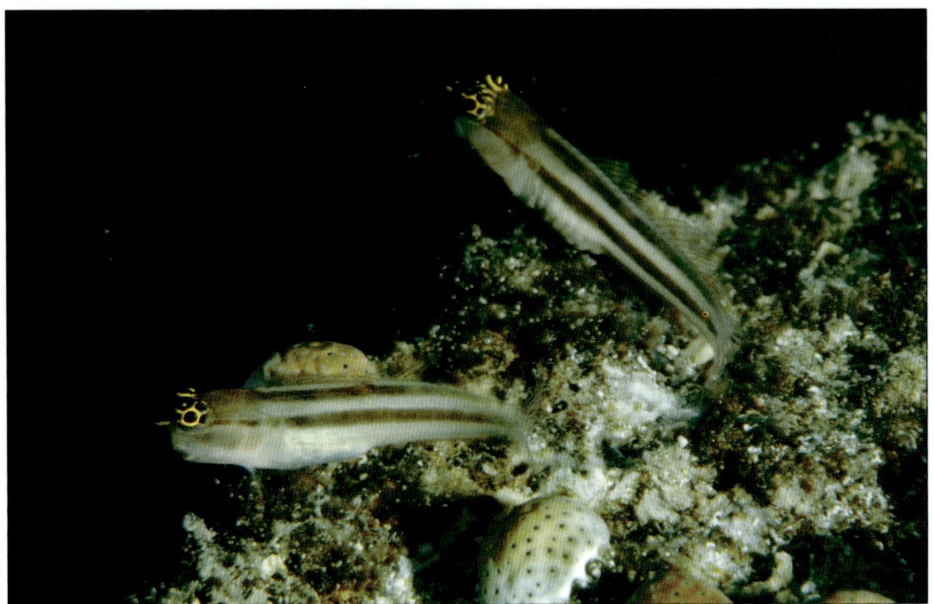

Gobies photographed with full strobe lighting. The photograph was made interesting by the paired fish and their yellow eyes. Neither fish is in the center of the frame. The negative space is black or nondescript dead coral that runs diagonally through the frame. **(Nikon F3; PKR; 105mm Micro Nikkor lens with 2x TC; Nikonos SB-105 and SB-103 strobes; 1/60 second at ƒ11)**

Sometimes, with 55mm or 60mm macrolenses the strobe must be placed almost vertically. Such lighting at an extreme angle produces high contrast and distinct shadows and the harsh, "high key" lighting effect.

The longer focal length provided by 105mm and 200mm macrolenses permits one to obtain 1: 2 or 1: 1 magnification ratios several inches from the subjects. This distance is enough to permit photography of skittish animals (e.g., tube worms) and allows the placement of strobes to the sides of the subject. This eliminates the need for high key lighting.

The length of macrolenses causes a bellows effect. As the lens is extended to focus closer and provide more magnification, the effective aperture decreases in size. Less light reaches the film plane. For example, at ƒ22 a fully extended macrolens can have an effective aperture of ƒ32 or even ƒ64, depending on the length of the lens. As the magnification ratio increases, one moves closer to the subject and the strobe to subject distance decreases. The result can be a single aperture used over a wide range of distances. This aperture can not be predicted from the information provided in strobe tables. One of the advantages of TTL exposure is that it compensates automatically for these unpredictable factors by measuring strobe light that hits the film plane.

Essentials of Underwater Photography

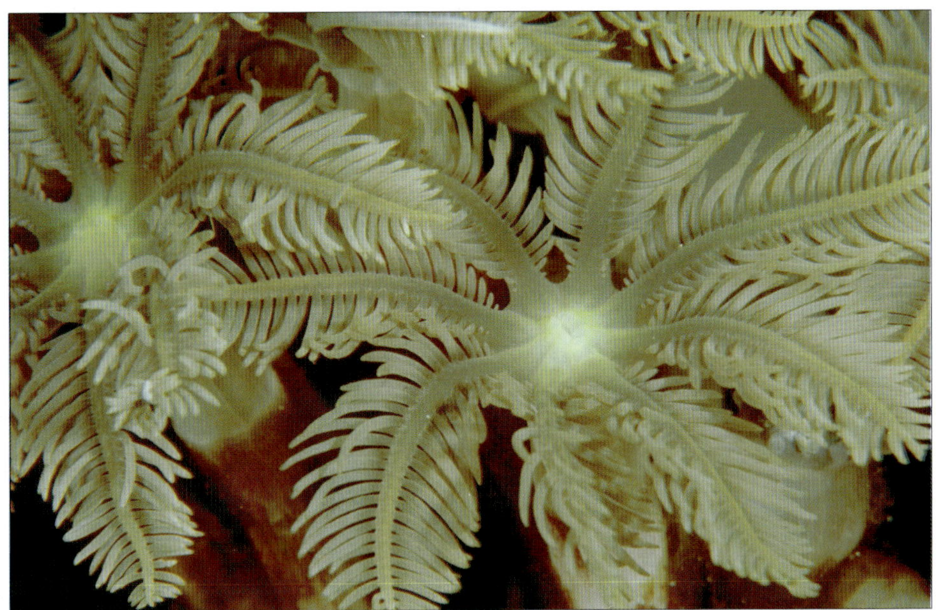

Octocoral macrophotograph. The points of interest are the centers of the octocorals, and these are set off from the frame. Since most of the flower-like structure was in a single plane, the focus is sharp. The lighting is quite even, as the strobes were balanced. **(Nikon F3; LPZ 100; 105mm Micro Nikkor lens with 1.4x TC; Nikonos SB-105 and SB-103 strobes; 1/60 second at ƒ16)**

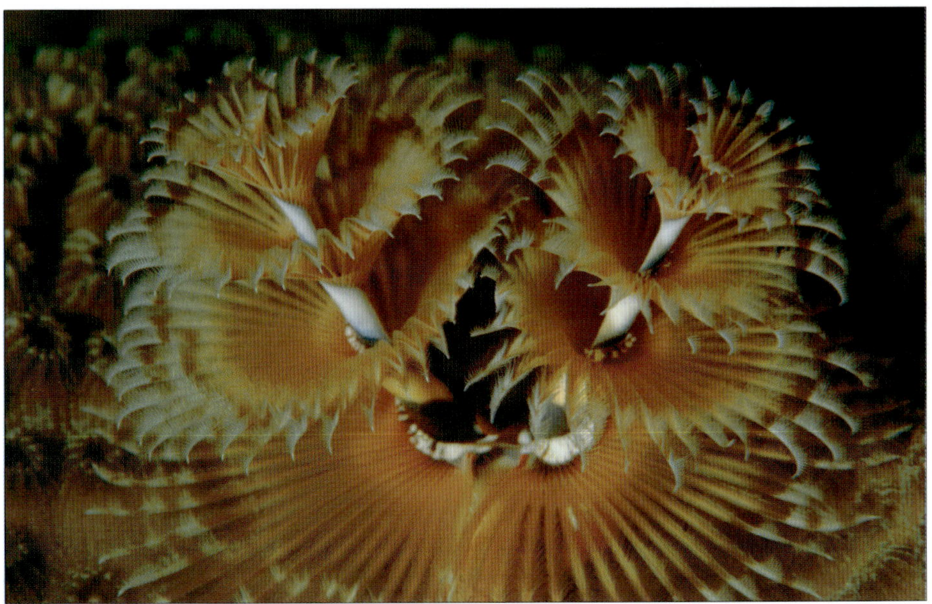

Serpulid worm in the Caribbean. Detail in the gills is sharp, although not all of the gills are in the plane of focus. Diagonal composition is suggested by the "V" formed by the two white radioles. **(Nikon F3; LPZ 100; 105mm Micro Nikkor lens with 2x TC; Nikonos SB-105 and SB-103 strobes; 1/60 second at ƒ11)**

Techniques

In many ways, close-up or macrophotography is the easiest kind of underwater photography. Many underwater photographers begin shooting close-up and macrophotographs and then graduate to more complex forms like wide-angle with flash-fill.

Close-up and macrophotography (by virtue of narrow depth of field at 1: 2 or 1: 1 magnification) allow the point of focus to define composition. **The point of focus does not need to be in the center of the image**. Autofocus cameras tend to focus on the center of the image. Focus should be set for the closest working distance. Small adjustments can be made based on subject size and composition.

Depth of field appears to decrease as focal length increases. For example, a 16mm lens appears to have a greater depth of field than a 200mm lens. It is the degree of magnification that determines the depth of field and at an equal magnification (say, 1: 4) a wide-angle lens and a telephoto lens will have the same "depth of field." The wide-angle lens will be much closer to the subject than the telephoto lens. Depth of field depends on focal length and distance, since they determine the degree of magnification. The focal length of the lens is an important factor, because camera-to-subject distance is often controlled by other factors.

Focusing a macrolens depends on adequate light on the subject and a large viewfinder. A Nikon Action Finder is a good example. Modern autofocus cameras and lenses can be used for macrophotography. Drawbacks include the need to focus on the center of the field of vision, the tendency of the lens to hunt for focus, and the need for strong light for the autofocus to work.

Essentials of Underwater Photography

"Some may regard me as crazy, but I must say these were the best and most fascinating times I ever experienced under water. When taking these pictures — and later when looking at the films — I became aware of details which I'd otherwise never have noticed. But the more you investigate the detail of nature, the finer points, the more astonishing and diverse are your discoveries. Purely from a physical aspect, taking these pictures was a climax for it demanded that my whole body adjust to the water, to every current and to every movement."
Hans Hass, 1973, <u>Men Beneath the Sea</u>

Over-under Shooting

This technique, if successful, results in the lower-half of the frame showing an underwater scene and the upper-half revealing the above-water scene. The result may be called "over-under," or "split-image" photography. The upper (air) part of the frame should be properly exposed and the lower (water) half of the frame clear, focused, and well lighted. This technique is difficult and requires specialized equipment.

Over-under shooting requires unique equipment. A housing with a <u>large diameter</u> dome port (6 - 8") is needed to allow the use of a wide-angle lens. Nikon lenses may be used with the Nikonos V (using a housing for these lenses produced by Aquatica), but this chapter concentrates on housed cameras only. The most important equipment is a wide-angle lens, usually ranging from 14mm to 17mm. Either a full frame fisheye or rectilinear lens can be used. The most commonly used lenses include the Sigma 14mm and the Nikon 16mm fisheyes. These have extremely wide depth of field, allowing them to focus simultaneously on the virtual image under water and on the actual image near infinity above water.

The next requirement, if the 16 or 14mm fisheye is not used, is a split close-up lens. The lens is physically cut in half. This is a 2+ or 3+ diopter, which allows lenses focused at infinity to focus on close objects. The virtual (underwater) image seems to be about 12 - 16" from the dome port. Obtaining correct exposure is a problem, given

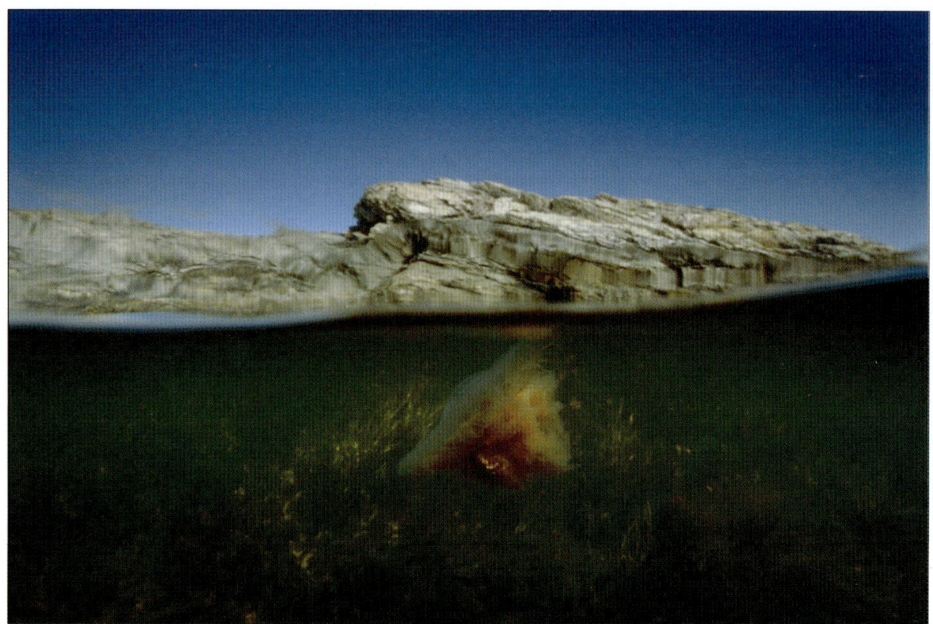

"Over-under" photograph showing a lion's mane jellyfish below the surface and a large rock and sky above. This photograph required preparation and is one of many attempts that resulted from bracketing all *f* stops and waiting for the decisive moment. **(Nikon F3; EPP at 200; 17mm lens with graduated neutral density filter (above) and 2+ diopter split lens (below); available light; 1/60 second at *f*4)**

the possible difference in light available above the surface compared to reduced light levels below.

The third requirement is a graduated neutral density filter. Usually, this is a 2 *f* stop neutral density filter, assuming the underwater scene would be correctly exposed at 2 stops more open than above water. For example, if the above water exposure is *f*11, the below water exposure would be *f*5.6. This is just an approximation and wide bracketing is needed to produce the final correctly exposed image. Split neutral density filters can also be obtained from Cokin (P series) and mounted as a unit with the split close-up lens.

At least one manufacturer now produces a combined, graduated neutral density filter and close-up diopter lens that screws into the prime lens filter threads. "Over-under" lenses take up less space than the Cokin filter units and are dedicated to use in underwater housings.

The basic procedure is to:

1. Attach the combined ND filter and close-up lens to the prime lens
   a. The darker part of the filter should be up
   b. The close-up diopter should below water

2.   Assemble the camera and housing
     a. Check for clearance
     b. Check for vignetting

3.   Focus manually on infinity or use the hyperfocal distance to include
     infinity
     a. The below-water part of the image should be in sharp focus

4.   Spread Rain-X® or another anti-wetting agent on the external dome
     surface

5.   Place the camera at the water surface, so that half of the dome is
     above and half is below water

6.   Bracket very widely

Photographing Pelagic Animals

Photography of sharks and mammals in the open ocean presents special challenges and opportunities. Success requires excellent diving skills and familiarity with photographic techniques.

Photography of large fishes (e.g., tuna) or mammals (e.g., dolphins) occurs in open water, possibly away from a visual reference to the bottom surface or vertical wall. This is usually done at or near the surface, so that breath hold diving may be used. Diving equipment should be limited to the essentials, e.g., mask, fins, snorkel, and camera equipment should be simple and as streamlined as possible.

A separate, narrow-angle light meter is important. The correct exposure will always be based on the blue water background as described in Chapter 3. The meter reading should be taken from the middle of the water column, at least 45 - 60° away from the sun. The meter should be aimed horizontally. The previously manufactured Sekonic Marine Meter was ideal. An SLR meter set on spot metering can be substituted.

A moderately wide-angle lens usually set at the hyperfocal distance is needed to capture rapidly moving animals with out taking time to focus. Although extreme wide-angle lenses (e.g., the Nikon 16mm fisheye) have great depth of field (because of their small degree of enlargement), less extreme wide-angle lenses may produce better results. Mammals often have a comfort zone and will not come closer than 1 - 2 meters. A moderate wide-angle lens allows a full frame portrait of a fairly distant subject. Lens choices include the Nikonos V with 20mm lens and the Nikkor 24 or 28mm lenses housed behind a dome port. A lens hood (shade) may help prevent extraneous light reflected from surfaces causing flares.

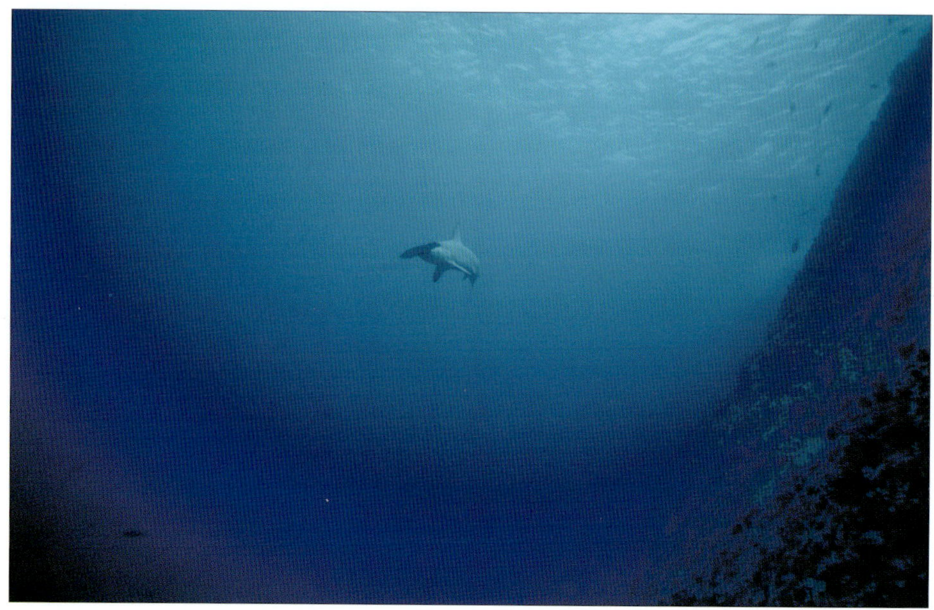

Hammerhead shark photographed at the surface. The shark swam close as I waited at the surface for pick up by the inflatable. I kept a Nikonos camera prefocused (at the hyperfocal distance) and set the aperture in preparation for such an opportunity. **(Nikonos V; PKL 200; 15mm lens; available light; 1/60 second at *f* 11)**

Housed cameras should be streamlined and neutrally buoyant. Strobes are often not needed and can be removed. They may impede movement through the water. If the strobes are used, they can be set to a power level below ambient light to provide fill in lighting, if the subject is close. The correct exposure will be controlled by the ambient light level as obtained from the blue water.

Recently, semi-closed circuit rebreathers have become available. These units produce fewer exhaust bubbles than the standard scuba regulator, and they may be useful for photographing animals that are frightened by bubbles. Rebreathers are especially useful when the pelagic animals being photographed do not swim at the surface.

The goal should be to produce properly exposed photographs based on the blue water background, in which the subject occupies a large portion of the frame area.

Shipwrecks

Wrecks can be photographed as objects, rather than as habitats for marine organisms. This requires recognition of the geometric form produced by the wreck and how those shapes interact with light in the water.

Essentials of Underwater Photography

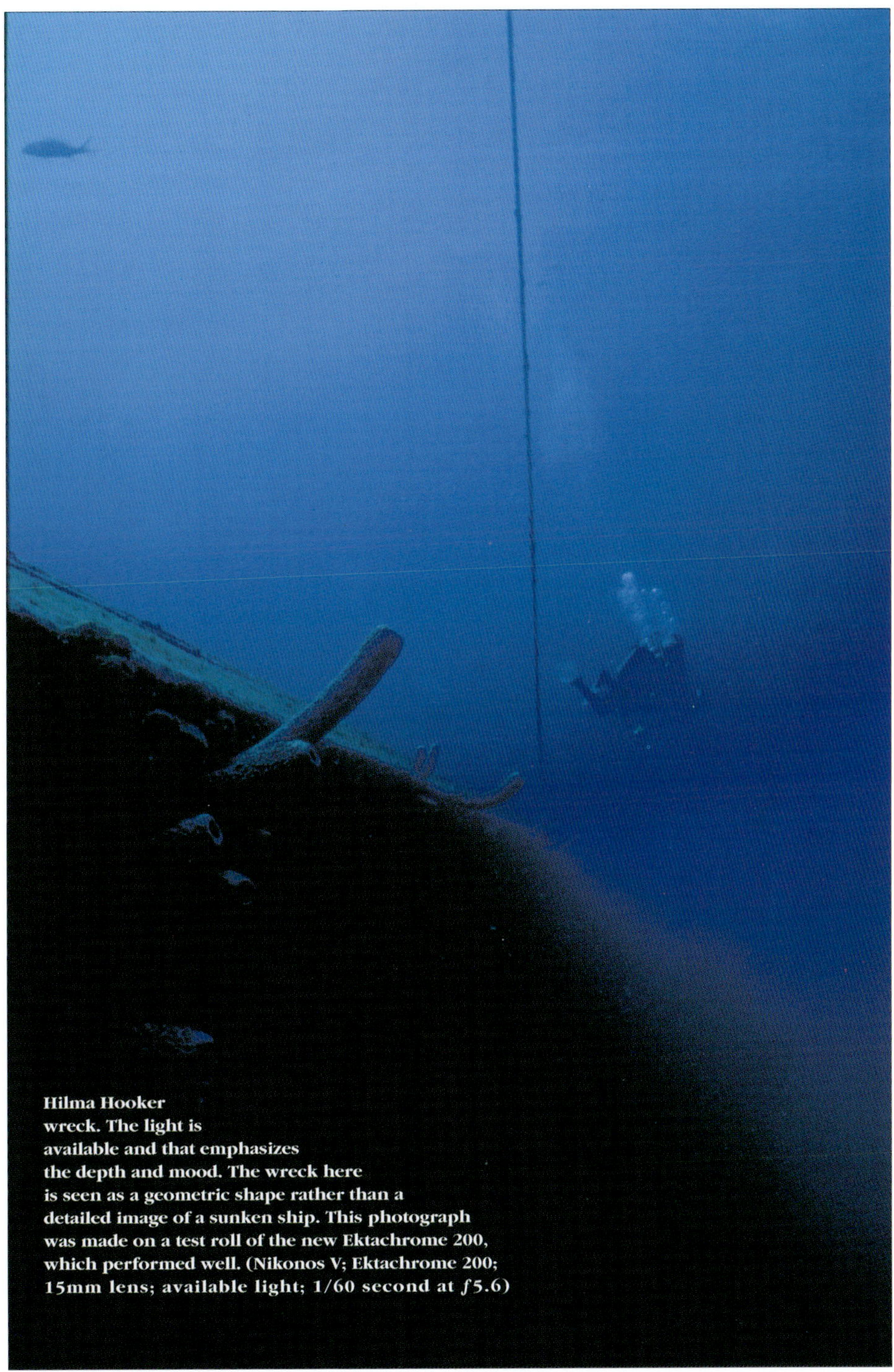

Hilma Hooker
wreck. The light is
available and that emphasizes
the depth and mood. The wreck here
is seen as a geometric shape rather than a
detailed image of a sunken ship. This photograph
was made on a test roll of the new Ektachrome 200,
which performed well. (Nikonos V; Ektachrome 200;
15mm lens; available light; 1/60 second at $f5.6$)

Photographing shipwrecks *per se* almost always requires a wide-angle lens. Available light is used to enhance contrast between light in the water and the dark form of the wreck or its pieces. A narrow angle light meter (e.g., the Sekonic Marine Meter), should be used to measure the midwater light levels. The amount of light may differ by four or more *f* stops from the top to the bottom of a wreck.

Strobe lighting can be used to illuminate foreground subjects or to provide fill-in lighting in shadow areas. Balancing sunlight and strobe light is much more difficult on a wreck (which is usually on the bottom, where ambient light is low) than it is near the surface, where ambient light is abundant.

Silhouetting wreck structures at an upward angle is the best technique. An extreme wide-angle lens, e.g., the Nikon 16mm, can be used effectively in this situation. Full frame fisheye lenses do not produce notable distortion when used far from the primary subject, because of the lack of straight lines as visual reference.

High contrast black and white film can be used to produce dramatic images. Even visible grain, due to pushing or enlargement, may enhance the effect. Close-up wide-angle techniques can also be used to photograph the details of a wreck.

Night Diving

Diving at night provides opportunities for photographing animals and behavior not normally seen during the day. Night eliminates ambient light from exposure calculations making the strobe the only source of exposure. This results in macrophotography with full strobe illumination. While this simplifies matters photographically, diving at night requires special care and equipment.

The camera equipment almost always consists of close-up or macrolenses on one or two strobes. Nikonos V cameras equipped with 1: 3, 1: 2, or 1: 1 extension tubes and framers can be used successfully in the dark, since they do not require much ambient light for focusing.

Macrolenses used at night commonly include the 60 and 105mm Micro Nikkor lenses, and less frequently, the 200mm Micro Nikkor. Focusing and aiming lights are required, and these can serve as the primary dive lights.

Focusing lights should be bright enough to allow autofocus to be used and to serve as the dive light. They should not be so bright that they frighten or stress light-sensitive creatures. Using a diffuser over the primary focusing light may minimize this effect.

                    Essentials of Underwater Photography

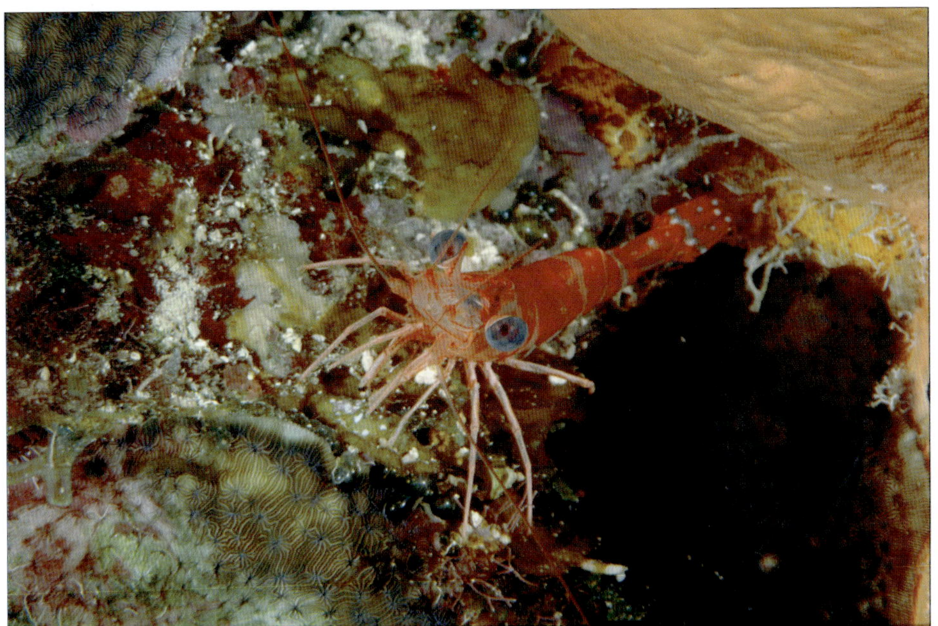

Nocturnal shrimp (note the large eyes). The focus is on the eyes, as is conventional in photographs of animals. The composition is diagonal to an extent. Although the photograph is looking down at the shrimp, it remains interesting because the shrimp seems to be looking back. **(Nikon F3; Velvia; 105mm lens; two Nikonos SB-103 strobes; 1/60 second at ƒ16)**

Since most photography at night uses full strobe illumination, slow, fine grain film can be used. Kodachrome 25, Velvia (ISO 40), Kodachrome 64, or E100S(W) film are all effective. Faster film shows more grain and produces greater contrast. Because full strobe illumination will be used, fast color films are not needed.

Diving photographers always should be equipped with a back up light and signaling equipment, like a flashing strobe or chemical light sticks. A sound source (whistle or Dive Alert) should also be carried.

Photography at night produces opportunities for photographing invertebrates like coral, mollusks, and shrimp. Little swimming should be required since subjects can be sought near the shore or boat. Frequently, one unusual opportunity can make a night dive, like finding a rare invertebrate and capturing it on film.

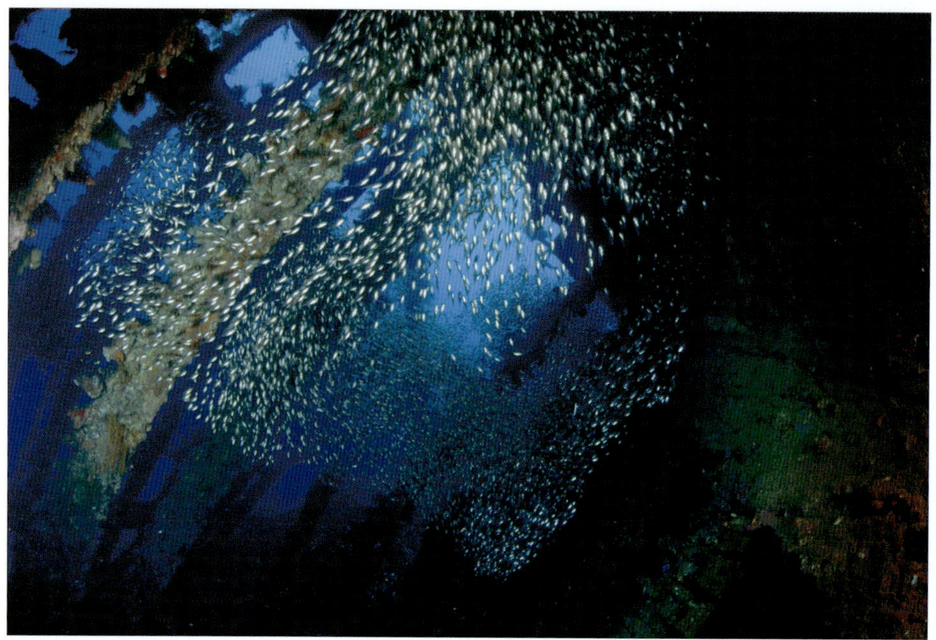

School of silversides photographed in the wreck of the Carnatic in the Red Sea. The wreck is in silhouette. The wide-angle lens makes the ribs appear curved, but they remain clearly visible as the school approaches the camera. In this photograph the ribs of the wreck make an abstract pattern in the background. **(Nikon F3; LPZ 100; available light with fill-in strobe; 16mm lens; two Sea and Sea YS-200 strobes on 1/2 power; 1/60 second at f5.6)**

PUTTING IT ALL TOGETHER

"Faulkner likes to push himself. He believes that no photographer works harder underwater. He is proud of the number of rolls he has shot by a given date and is obsessed with the number he has yet to shoot. He sets goals for each day's diving."
  Kenneth Brower, 1974, <u>With Their Islands Around Them</u>

Previsualization

The final step in underwater photography is to apply your knowledge using real equipment to dynamic situations in the ocean. This chapter provides some suggested approaches. Successful application of these techniques should lead to making underwater photographs, rather than simply taking snapshots of targets of opportunity.

Previsualization is an important step in the process of making a successful underwater photograph. Previsualization implies developing a mental image of the photograph to be taken. Developing a concept of the photograph to be made allows choice of film, lenses, and other equipment to be made most efficiently. One could draw the image on paper so elements of composition are arranged and perspective chosen in advance. Previsualization means the photographer imagines himself in the situation, and it permits imaginary rearrangement and repositioning of all the elements of composition. Previsualization is a form of mental rehearsal and instills confidence. The photographer has the opportunity to arrange elements of the photograph and vary composition before attempting the photograph.

Buoyancy and Other Adjustments

An underwater photographer has the ability to move and alter perspective in three dimensions. Keeping appropriate buoyancy allows easy movement in all directions. Photographs taken in midwater require neutral buoyancy so that the photographer can hang motionless, without exerting energy. Neutral buoyancy is achieved by adding or removing weights, so the diver neither sinks nor rises at the end of a dive with a nearly empty tank. Buoyancy can be adjusted at the surface, so that the diver sinks slowly from the surface (i.e., the diver starts the dive with slight negative buoyancy). An underwater photographer usually carries a heavy camera strobe unit that may itself be negatively buoyant. Weight may need to be removed to maintain neutral buoyancy. Photography may require the photographer find a position in which he can stay with minimal movement. This may be on the sand bottom to maintain slight up looking perspective while shooting. In this situation, negative buoyancy is needed to stay there.

Attaining a comfortable position in the water requires neutral buoyancy, while finding a stable position on the bottom requires slight negative buoyancy. In either case, the diver should be free to move into a comfortable position. The "compositional" position is the final essential element required for composing the photograph.

The photographer should adjust buoyancy as required, and mentally compose and rehearse the photograph to attain the correct position for the composition. Finally, using breath control to remain motionless, the photographer makes the photograph.

Attention to detail is important to the successful creation of a photograph. Dangling gauges should be removed from the frame. Small air leaks (e.g., from a regulator) should be stopped, before the bubbles leak into the shot. Bubbles should be removed from the dome or flat port. Exhale prior to composing, if necessary, inhale quietly while making the photograph. This will minimize disturbance to fish or other animals sensitive to the sound of bubbles.

All photographs should be bracketed to optimize chances for a successful shot. Exposure, focus, and composition should *all* be bracketed. Exposures can be bracketed in 1/3 to 1/2 f stop increments by changing aperture (manual cameras), or changing the ISO speed dial (automatic cameras). Flash power can be bracketed by changing strobe power, using a diffuser (manual), or by changing the ISO setting (TTL). Simply moving the strobe back and forth to change the strobe-to-subject distance is another effective technique for bracketing strobe exposures. Finally, composition and focusing can be bracketed by slightly moving the camera each time the photograph is repeated. Very wide bracketing of exposures may be necessary because conditions are changing rapidly, or the range of exposure values in the scene is extremely wide.

                                        Essentials of Underwater Photography

Handling Cameras at Sea

Handling equipment on boats is necessary to photograph in most locations. Working from boats makes U/W photography easier, but presents some specialized challenges. Extra care must be taken to prevent damage to camera equipment while at sea. All delicate equipment should be stowed as low as possible on the deck, so it really has nowhere to fall. Lenses and other equipment should be kept in soft cases within boxes. Camera housings and attached strobes are usually kept on a camera table in the open on the stern deck. Often the camera table is surfaced with carpeting to prevent damage and to prevent small parts from rolling away. Hair and face should be dried before opening camera housings so that water does not drip in the camera. Compressed air should not be used to dry surfaces because it can spread water over large areas. Threaded strobe connections should not be left screwed together for a long period of time. Water can enter the threads and cause pitting of the metal surfaces, if they are not cleaned free of salt water daily and lubricated with silicone grease. Dome ports should always be protected using rubber covers or soft towels. Housings should be placed in a stable, back down position, so they do not roll or fall forward on the dome. **Equipment should always be kept out of the sun**, which can seriously damage plastics by UV light and overheat mechanical and electrical components.

Cameras, strobes, and housings should always be assembled well in advance of the first photographic dive. Housings can be assembled without strobes and tested for leaks at depth. Camera housings should be handled carefully by the boat staff. The photographer may need to instruct the boat staff in proper handling. Housings should be held and carried by the handles (not the strobe arms). Housings should be placed in the water with the dome down, so that leaks can be seen and water can be kept away from the camera itself. The photographer can look into the dome port during descent and ascend if water appears in the dome.

Failures, floods, and other catastrophes can and do happen. Although such failures are inevitable, one cannot predict when they will occur. Constant vigilance is required. Some problems can be corrected in the field. Multiple copies of critical spare parts and a repair kit allows replacement of non-functioning electrical components. A field repair manual is beyond the scope of this book, but excellent handbooks do exist. It is often possible to save flooded Nikonos cameras by rinsing in fresh (preferably distilled) water and drying in low heat (in engine rooms). Mechanical cameras like the Nikonos III are much more robust than electronic cameras and survive floods more easily.

Traveling

Almost all diving and underwater photography requires travel to distant locations. This requires logistic planning to ensure successful arrival of all equipment at the dive site. Overweight baggage is an inevitable problem for which the underwater photographer should be prepared. Extra charges are frequently involved and usually require cash payment in local currency. Worse, some small aircraft simply cannot carry all of the weight required to take underwater photographers to the distant locations. In this case, advance planning may help.

Travel can be started several days early to optimize chances of gear getting aboard a flight. To some locations administered by the US, shipment by USPS or UPS may be a possible option (e.g., Bikini Atoll, Micronesia). Otherwise, stripping gear to the essentials may be necessary. Some equipment can be carried on a photographer's vest and it may be possible to escape a baggage weight limit using this technique.

Packing efficiently is essential and can prevent breaking equipment during transport. Rigid plastic or fiberglass shipping containers are best. Those with wheels are most useful, since filled containers are frequently heavy. Hard-sided Styrofoam coolers are preferred by some photographers because of their light weight. Styrofoam also provides a degree of protection from shock. Securing the cover of the cooler can be done with duct tape, or more permanent closures can be constructed from metal.

Packing should not be done with foam rubber or other materials. This just takes up space and provides minimal protection. Rather, equipment should be packed as close together as possible. Towels, tee shirts and other clothing is used to wrap strobes and other delicate items. Any unused space can be filled with unexposed film in double lead bags or other small pieces of equipment. Another secret of packing is to secure heavy pieces of equipment to the shipping case. This can be accomplished by drilling a 17/64" hole through the case wall and using a 1/4" stainless steel bolt to secure the housing through the tripod mounting screws present in the bottom of the housing.

A

AE (Automatic Exposure) Programmed auto exposure, aperture-priority auto exposure, and shutter-priority auto exposure.

AE (Automatic Exposure) Lock Used to hold an automatically controlled shutter speed and/or lens aperture.

AF-I Lens with built-in autofocus drive motor. CPU is also built in. AF-I Nikkor lenses send information on distance to the camera body and are classified as D-type AF Nikkor lenses.

AI (Automatic Index) Nikon's system for telling the camera's exposure meter the lens' maximum aperture.

AI/S (Automatic Index/Shutter) Nikon's lens-mount permitting automatic operation in shutter-priority and program auto-exposure systems.

Aperture The variable opening produced by the iris-diaphragm through which light passes to the film plane. Measured in f stops.

Aperture Priority Autoexposure systems wherein the photographer selects the aperture and the camera selects the appropriate shutter speed.

APO (Apochromatic) A type of lens which focuses different wavelengths of light on the film plane for improved image sharpness. Chromatic aberration is corrected.

Aspheric A lens design incorporating elements ground so the curve of the surface does not describe an arc of a circle. Especially useful in reducing distortion in wide-angle lenses.

ASA (American Standardization Association) One of several units of measure for the speed of films. Doubling or halving the ASA value is equivalent to doubling or halving the film speed.

B

B (Bulb) At the B setting, the shutter remains open as long as the shutter release button remains fully depressed.

Bracketing Taking a series of pictures at different exposures.

C

Catadioptric A lens built with a combination of mirrors and elements. The light path is folded by the mirror surfaces, permitting a reduction in overall length and weight compared with conventional lenses of equivalent focal lengths.

Chromatic Aberration Light rays passing through a lens focus at different points, depending on the wavelength of the light.

Coating Layer or multiple layers of thin anti-reflective materials applied to the surface of lens elements to reduce light reflection (flare) and increase the amount of transmitted light.

Close-Up The general term for pictures taken at relatively close distances, from 1/10 life-size (1:10) to life-size (1:1).

Color The sensation of "color" only comes about after a complex operation in which the brain processes the information relating to the incoming stimuli. The photoreceptors of the retina (rods and cones) convert light into nerve impulses. Three kinds of cones with different sensitivities for different wavelengths are responsible for color vision, i.e., responding to stimuli in the visible spectrum.

D

DIN, ASA, and ISO speeds Different systems are used for stating the film speed: the arithmetic ASA system and the logarithmic DIN system. Doubling or halving the photographic speed is equivalent to doubling or halving the ASA number in the ASA system or raising or lowering the DIN number by three units in the DIN system. Both speed systems are combined in the international ISO standard:

25 ASA	100 ASA	400 ASA
15 DIN	21 DIN	27 DIN
ISO 25/15°	ISO 100/21°	ISO 400/27°

DIN speed The absolute measure of the speed of black-and-white negative films.

DX code An electronically readable information system for 35mm films. Code enables DX cameras to automatically control film speed and to identify exposure latitude and number of exposures. The checkered code consists of two rows of electronically conductive (silver colored) and non-conductive (black) rectangles. The electronically readable cartridge bar code provides processing information for automatic identification of the manufacturer, the process, the film type, the film speed, and the film length.

Depth of Field The range of acceptably sharp focus in front of and behind the distance the lens is focused at.

Diaphragm A series of metal "blades" that can be manipulated to form a larger or smaller opening through which the light is admitted.

E

EI (Exposure Index) A number representing any combination of aperture and shutter speed which will provide "correct" exposure for a particular situation. (See EV).

Element One piece of glass comprising the internal optics of a lens.

EV (Exposure Value) A number that represents available combinations of shutter speed and aperture offering the same exposure effect when scene brightness remains the same.

Exposure Light striking a sensitized material (film or paper emulsion).

Exposure Compensation Modifying the shutter speed and/or lens aperture recommended by the camera's light meter in order to produce special creative effects or to meet special requirements.

Edge Effect The rendition of the light-to-dark transition of an edge (e.g., a line screen) exposed on a photographic material characterizes the sharpness. The edge or contour sharpness of that material.

F

Fill-in Flash Exposure consisting of a combination of flash and "available light" balanced to produce an even mix of the two.

Fisheye An ultra-wide-angle lens which purposely introduces barrel distortion so straight lines near the edges of the frame appear to curve out.

Flare Image degradation caused by stray light that passes through the lens but is not focused to form the primary image. Often caused by light bouncing off internal air-to-glass surfaces.

Focal Length The distance from the optical center of a lens to the image plane when the lens is focused to infinity.

G

Group Two or more elements cemented together within a lens. Lenses are described as having a certain number of elements in a smaller number of groups.

Guide Number The power of a flash in relation to ISO film speed. Guide numbers are quoted in either meters or feet (to convert from meters to feet, multiply the metric number by 3.3). Guide numbers are used to calculate the f stop for correct exposure as follows: f stop = guide number/distance.

Graininess The term grain is generally taken to mean a single silver halide crystal. The sum of all the grains in the various light-sensitive layers produces the image-forming structure. Comparisons of granularity are carried out using the root mean square method (RMS).

H

Hot Shoe A mounting device, usually built onto the top of a camera, that enables a flash unit, or speedlight, to be mounted on and triggered by the camera.

Hyperfocal Distance The distance setting on a lens which affords the maximum depth of field for a given aperture (*f* stop). The closest point of focus where the depth of field includes infinity.

I

IF (Internal Focus) A focus system wherein lens elements or groups move within the lens barrel, but the barrel length remains fixed and the front element does not rotate.

ISO (International Standards Organization) The number represents the film's sensitivity to light. A higher ISO number indicates the film is more sensitive and requires less light for a proper exposure.

L

Latitude The variance from "proper" exposure that will still provide acceptable results.

Layer Structure Color materials are made up of a base with three differently sensitized emulsion layers (which in turn can consist of several part-layers) plus a number of auxiliary layers, such as protective layers, active interlayers, adhesive layers, anti-halation layers, filter layers, and anti-static layers. In the case of color materials, the top blue-sensitive emulsion layer has a yellow coupler; the middle, green-sensitive layer has a magenta coupler; and the bottom red-sensitive layer has a cyan coupler.

Light Electromagnetic radiation within the spectral range that can be perceived by the human eye. The visible range extends from approximately 380 to 760nm (nanometer). Photographic materials for taking pictures are sensitized for the range of visible light (sensitization).

Logarithms The logarithm of a number to a given base is the power to which the base must be raised to produce the number. For example, the logarithm of 64 to the base 8 is 2 (82 = 8 x 8 = 64). Logarithms to the base 10 can be recognized from the generally written shortened form, lg or log 10.

M

Matrix Autoexposure metering where the camera sets both aperture and shutter speed according to data stored in the camera's built-in memory, comparing the scene to be photographed to reference scenes.

Macrofocusing Macrofocusing, applied to zoom lenses, moves the lens-group(s), enabling the lens to focus closer than the normal focusing distance from close-up shooting.

Macro The picture-taking range from near life-size (1: 3) to 2x (2: 1) magnification.

Micrometer (uM) A physical unit of length equivalent to 10-6 meters, i.e. one thousandth of a millimeter.

N

Nanometer (nm) A physical unit of length equal to meters, i.e. a billionth of a meter or a millionth of a millimeter.

O

OTF (Off The Filmplane) A metering system which measures the light bouncing off the film, rather than simply measuring the light entering the lens. Often coupled with TTL for automated flash exposure.

P

PC (Positive Connection) Connection from camera body to a flash that is not fired from the hot shoe.

Process Compatibility Photographic materials are process-compatible if they can be processed by the specified processes from that particular manufacturer and by the process specified for comparable materials from other companies without any depreciation in quality. For this reason, the processing times, temperatures, and tolerances of compatible processes correspond with each other.

R

Reproduction Ratio The size of the image recorded on film divided by the actual size of the subject. This term is used in close-up or macrophotography to express the magnification of a subject. As a general rule, for subjects located farther away from the camera, the reproduction ratio equals the lens focal length divided by the shooting distance. For example, a 200mm lens divided by two meters would produce a 1:10 reproduction ratio.

Resolution The ability of a lens or photographic material to reproduce small details; measured in lines per millimeter.

Reciprocity Failure With very long exposure times, the relative speed of the materials declines while at the same time, the gradation becomes steeper.

Resolving Power The resolving power — or resolution — of a photographic emulsion layer describes the ability of a material to reproduce the finest adjacent details (e.g., lines in a line screen). Visual criterion for the image quality of a photographic material (nevertheless based on standardized photographic and physical testing conditions). The maximum resolving power of a photographic material describes the number of lines per millimeter.

RMS Method for measuring the granularity of a photographic material. On enlargement, granularity becomes evident as an uneven structuring of grey and color densities. The granularity of films can either be compared visually (usually with the aid of 12x enlargements of comparative prints) or by measurement.

S

Shutter Priority Autoexposure systems in which the photographer selects the shutter speed and the camera selects the appropriate aperture.

SLR (Single Lens Reflex) Viewer and film "see" through the same lens via a system of mirror and prism

Spectral Sensitivity The sensitivity (sensitization) of photographic materials to certain spectral components of visible light is known as the spectral sensitivity. In their optically unsensitized state, photographic emulsions have the property of being sensitive to only one part of visible light (up to approximately 510nm). The silver halides can also be made sensitive to green and red light by means of special organic dyes (spectral sensitizes), which are adsorbed on the surface of the silver halide crystals.

T

T (Time) At the T setting, the shutter remains open until, for example, it is closed by rotating the shutter speed dial, etc.

TTL (Through The Lens) Viewing (or more commonly metering) through the picture-taking lens.

U

Ultra Short Time Effect With photographic materials, very short exposure times combined with high light intensities result in a loss of speed, contrast, and color shifts.

W

Working Distance The distance from the front of the lens surface to the subject. The more frequently used term "shooting distance" refers to the distance between the subject and the filmplane. Working distance is most often used in close-up photography, especially when shooting a shy subject, such as a fish, or when the lens may hamper lighting.

X

X-sync The maximum (fastest) shutter speed at which electronic flash pictures may be taken.

EQUIPMENT & SERVICES

ABSea Photo
9136 Sepulveda Blvd.
Los Angeles, CA 90045
USA
Tel: 310-645-8992
Fax: 310-645-3645
www.absea.net
info@absea.net

Aqua Vision Systems
"Aquatica" Aluminum SLR Housings
7730 Trans Canada Highway
Montréal, Québec
Canada H4T 1A5
Tel: 888-737-9481 or 514-737-9481
Fax: 514-737-7685
www.aquatica.ca
aquatica@aquatica.ca

B & H Photo
420 9th Ave.
New York, NY 10001
USA
Tel: 800-947-6628 or 212-444-6608
Fax: 800-947-7008 or 212-242-1400
photo@bhphotovideo.com
www.bhphotovideo.com

Backscatter U/W Video & Photo
32 Cannery Row
Monterey, CA 93940
Tel: 408-645-1082
Fax: 408-375-1526
www.backscatter.com
sales@backscatter.com

Beattie Camera
2407 Guthrie Ave.
Cleveland, TN 37311
USA
Tel: 800-251-6333
www.beattiesystems.com
webmaster@beattiesystems.com

Camera Tech
2308 Taraval St
San Francisco, CA, 94121
Tel: 415-387-1700
Fax: 415242-1719
www.cameratech.com
info@cameratech.com

Gates Underwater Products
Camera Housings & Custom Work
5111 Santa Fe St, Suite H
San Diego, CA, 92109
USA
Tel: 800-875-1052 or 619-272-2501
Fax: 619-272-1208
www.gateshousings.com
info@gateshousings.com

Hasselblad
USA Distributor
Victor Hasselblad Inc.
10 Madison Rd
Fairfield, NJ, 07004
USA
Tel: 201-227-7320
www.hasselblad.com
info@hasselblad.se

Helix Photo
310 S. Racine Ave
Chicago, IL, 60607
USA
Tel: 800-33HELIX
Tel: (In Illinois) 312-421-6000
Fax: 312-421-2804
www.helixcamera.com
helix4uw@aol.com

Hugyfot
Aluminum SLR Housings
D-78333 Stockach-Bodensee
Höllestrasse 4
Germany
Tel: ++49(0) 7771-62211
Fax: ++49(0) 7771-62230
www.hugyfot.de
hugyfot@hugyfot.de

Ikelite
50 W. 33rd St
Indianapolis, IN, 46208
USA
Tel: 317-923-4523
Fax: 317-924-7988
www.ikelite.com
ikelite@aol.com   or ikelite@
ikelite.com

Light & Motion Industries, Inc.
"Infinity" flexible strobe arms
300 Cannery Row
Monterey, CA, 93940
USA
Tel: 408-645-1525
Fax: 408-375-2517

MCD - Marine Camera
Distributors
"MCD" Strobes
11717 Sorrento Valley Rd
San Diego, CA, 92121
USA
Tel: 858-481-0604
Fax: 858-481-6499
www.marinecamera.com
mcd2000@marinecamera.com

Nexus
Various distributors
Housings for Nikon 6006, 8008,
N90, F4
www.nexusamerica.com
info@NexusAmerica.com

Nikon USA
Tel: 800-Nikon35
www.nikonusa.com

Pacific Camera Service
Service for Nikonos
Nikonos Accessories
Water detection alarm
2980 McClintock, Unit H
Costa Mesa, CA, 92626
USA
Tel: 949-642-7800
pac-cam@pacbell.net

Sea & Sea
1938 Kellogg Avenue
Carlsbad, CA, 92008
USA
Tel: 760-929-1909
Fax: 760-929-0098
www.seaandsea.com

SEACAM
Postfach 91
A-8570 Voitsberg
Austria
Tel: +43-3142-228850
Fax: +43-3142-228854
www.seacam.com
office@seacam.com

Sea Optics USA, Inc
201 S. Milpas St. #103
Santa Barbara, CA 93103
USA
Tel: 800-480-8333 or 805-965-5050
Fax: 805-965-3010
www.seaoptic.com
seaopticus@aol.com

Subal Underwater Housings
Aluminum SLR Housings for F4,
N90, N8008
P.O. Box 41609
Santa Barbara, CA 93140
Tel: 805-566-0756
Fax: 805-566-0856
www.subalusa.com
info@subalusa.com

Ultra Light Control Systems
Strobe Arms
3304 Ketch Avenue
Oxnard, CA 93035
USA
Tel: 800-635-6611 or 805-984-9104
Fax: 805-984-3008
www.ulcs.com
info@ulcs.com

Underwater Photo-Tech
Nikonos Service & Accessories
16 Manning St, Suite 104
Derry, NH, 03038
USA
Tel: 603-432-1997
Fax: 603-432-4702
www.uwphoto.com
sales@uwphoto.com

Kodachrome
Processing Laboratories

UNITED STATES
Kodak Premium Processing
P.O. Box 7000
Fair Lawn, NJ 07410-7000
Tel: 800-345-6973

A & I Color Lab
933 N. Highland Avenue
Los Angeles, CA 90038
Tel: 213-856-5255
Tel: 800-883-9088 (outside CA)
Fax: 213-856-0351

BWC Chrome Lab
233 11th Street
Miami Beach, FL 33139
Tel: 305-534-4454
Tel: 800-292-3664
Fax: 305-534-8833

AUSTRALIA
Vision Graphics Pty Ltd.
88 Pitt Street
Redfern, New South Wales 2016
AUSTRALIA
Tel: (61) (2) 319-3300
Fax: (61) (2) 699-8801

SWITZERLAND
Kodak SA
Processing Laboratories
Cas Postale Ch-1001 Lausanne
SWITZERLAND
Tel: (41) (21) 631-0111
Fax: (41) (21) 631-0150

UNITED KINGDOM
**KODACHROME Professional
Film Processing Laboratory**
29 Deer Park Road
Wimbledon, London
SW193UG, ENGLAND
Tel: (44) (081) 544-0055
Fax: (44) (081) 544-1493 or
(44) (081) 540-0794

JAPAN
Horiuchi Color Lab
1-6-7, Wada Suginami-Ku
Tokyo 166
JAPAN
Tel: (81) 03-3383-3321
FAX : (81) 03-3382-7493

KR Center
1320 Nishibori, Urawa
Saitama 338
JAPAN
Tel: (81) 048-864-5572
Fax : (81) 048-864-5575

INDEX

ACKNOWLEDGMENTS

Many people have contributed knowingly or not to my completion of this book. Inevitably omitting many, I thank especially: My mother, V.L. Jackson, for enrolling me in a YMCA scuba course; K. Adams, A. Barnaby, S. Major, K. Pacheco, M. Parker and J. Silverstein for unwavering logistical support; J. Church, C. Newbert and B. Wilms for their photographic insights; and M.J. Cramer and S.M. Harding for special help. Any success is as much theirs as mine.

—Robert M. Jackson

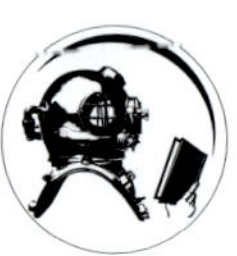